# SUICIDAL
# ADOLESCENTS

# SUICIDAL ADOLESCENTS

*By*

## PATRICIA A. DAVIS, M.S.E.

*University of Kansas*
*Lawrence, Kansas*

*With a Foreword by*

**Charles Neuringer, Ph.D.**

*Professor of Psychology*
*University of Kansas*
*Lawrence, Kansas*

**CHARLES C THOMAS • PUBLISHER**
*Springfield • Illinois • U.S.A.*

*Published and Distributed Throughout the World by*

CHARLES C THOMAS • PUBLISHER

2600 South First Street

Springfield, Illinois 62717

© *1983 by* CHARLES C THOMAS • PUBLISHER

ISBN 0-398-04866-5

Library of Congress Catalog Card Number: 83-4766

*Printed in the United States of America*
Q-R-3

*Library of Congress Cataloging in Publication Data*

Davis, Patricia A.
    Suicidal adolescents.

    Bibliography: p.
    Includes index.
       1. Youth — United States — Suicidal behavior.
    2. Suicide — United States — Prevention. I. Title.
    HV6546.D39  1983    362.2    83-4766
    ISBN 0-398-04866-5

*To my parents, Florence and Maloy*

# FOREWORD

## ADOLESCENT SUICIDE: THE CRISIS HAS ARRIVED

AT the 1967 convention of The International Association for Suicide Prevention, there appeared a theme not in evidence at earlier meetings. That previously unnoticed (or at least unmentioned) subject was that of increasing suicide in young people. At that meeting cries of alarm were sounded because hard evidence was presented that self-destruction among adolescents had suddenly reached near epidemic proportions. It had long been known that suicide was the second leading cause of death in young people, behind that of automobile accident deaths. But the recent sharp increase in self-inflicted death among this group led to a situation where the amelioration of adolescent suicide is now one of the major project goals of both *The International Association for Suicide Prevention* and *The American Association of Suicidology*. Whole issues of various journals have been dedicated to reports and discussion of this phenomenon.

The present writer has reported that suicide among adolescents, especially females, has risen dramatically in the last ten years. There were in the United States 4,000 or so self-inflicted deaths among adolescents last year. The extent of the problem can be best appreciated if these numbers are transformed into deaths per time units. When this is done, it yields eleven adolescent suicide deaths per day (or one such death every two and a quarter hours). All investigators in this area agree that the number of deaths recorded is a conservative estimate. Our knowledge of this number of suicide attempts among adolescents is less precise than is the information about suicidal adolescent deaths. Some experts have set the number of adolescent suicide attempts at close to 200,000 per annum. *The adolescent suicide epidemic crisis is now here.*

The suicide of a young person evokes in us a greater sense of futility and waste than does comparable suicidal behavior in older people. The mythologies of our society hold that youth and adolescence are supposed to be the golden, carefree time that precedes taking on the burdens of "adulthood." We are then profoundly shocked and moved by any situation that involves an adolescent finding life insupportable. Concern with the problem of adolescent suicide is certainly justified from humanitarian motives, but even more frightening is the evidence that adolescent suicide is still on the rise. This may be one of the early warning signs of the possible dissolution of the social fabric.

There are many causes for the upsurge of suicidal behavior in adolescents. Some of these relate to the disintegration of the nuclear family and the greater availability and abuse of drugs by adolescents. (Unfortunately, adolescents' most frequently used method of self-destructive behavior is through the medium of drug abuse.) It is reasonable to predict that the upsurge of suicidal behavior in adolescents has not yet reached its peak.

Interacting with the aforementioned causes is a national economic situation, which will, for many adolescents, preclude the pursuit of meaningful careers and economic self-sufficiency. One expects that feelings of hopelessness will increasingly spread to adolescents in segments of our society that have previously escaped "the loss of the American Dream." There may be little to distinguish between the adolescents of middle America and those of the ghetto.

For these reasons, Patricia Davis's book is especially welcome. There is no previous work that so thoroughly reviews what is known about suicidal adolescents. I know of no other book that offers parents and mental health workers insights into the dynamics of adolescent suicide, hints for early recognition, and suggestions for constructive procedures to avoid a tragedy. I feel very strongly that the volume you hold in your hands should be in every library, on every parent's bookshelf, and on every mental health worker's desk.

Charles Neuringer

# PREFACE

A DOLESCENT suicide has become an alarming national tragedy. The annual number of both attempted suicides and committed suicides by adolescents is growing at a frightening rate. Yet, this horrible tragedy continues to receive little attention.

While investigators agree there are few "absolutes" about suicide, one fact is certain. Ignoring this problem will not make it disappear.

However, before we can respond to this problem of great magnitude and complexity, we must first understand more fully the dynamics of suicidal behavior.

Upon researching the scattered literature on adolescent suicide, I discovered that there was no single comprehensive resource. The need to gather such information in a book became readily apparent; thus, my motivation for writing *Suicidal Adolescents*.

My goal in writing this book was to provide a comprehensive resource to caregivers, parents, and others in contact with adolescents, affording them the opportunity not only to become aware of the adolescent suicide problem but also how to recognize and respond to suicidal behavior.

*Suicidal Adolescents* begins with a historical perspective on the changing social attitudes toward suicide and an informative overview of the general topic of suicide. The book continues by examining the motivation and causes underlying suicidal behavior and reviewing the prodromal clues and treatment options as well as the processes of prevention, intervention, and postvention. The book concludes with a list of recommendations for those who live and work with adolescents. An extensive list of references provides an excellent research tool.

My book offers practical advice to caregivers, parents, and others in contact with adolescents. Educators will find this book an invaluable tool in teaching students and future caregivers about adolescent suicide.

Since even serious suicidal adolescents are ambivalent about death — that is, they vacillate between wanting to live and wanting to die up to the last moment — they send out many warning signals (which I refer to in the book as prodromal clues) that, if detected and recognized, would allow others to save them. However, those around them must be able to recognize these clues and know how to respond in order to save these adolescents.

With this book, *Suicidal Adolescents*, I believe caregivers, parents, and others in contact with adolescents can take the first step toward addressing this tragedy; they can obtain a better understanding of suicidal behavior in adolescents and learn how to recognize and respond to this type of behavior in adolescents.

I firmly believe that many adolescent suicide attempts can be prevented and the lives of many adolescents can be saved if caregivers, parents, and others in the lives of adolescents have the information that I have chosen to include in this book.

P.A.D.

# INTRODUCTION

ALTHOUGH I never had the opportunity to know my paternal grandfather as I was growing up (he died when my father was only four years old),it never occurred to me to ask my parents how he died. While there were family discussions about Grandmother and Grandfather Davis, the circumstances of my grandfather's death were never discussed.

However, a few years ago my mother disclosed to me that my grandfather had committed suicide. Although I was somewhat shocked to learn the circumstances of his death, I found it interesting that my mother and father had chosen to protect their children from this information.

I believe this experience typifies how suicidal behavior is frequently handled in our society; it is both concealed and denied. However, we can no longer allow the topic of adolescent suicide to be taboo. Statistics on adolescent suicide demand an immediate response to this national tragedy.

Adolescent suicide has become an alarming national tragedy. In the United States, suicides by adolescents have doubled in the past decade and tripled in the past two decades. The number continues to grow. When the number of attempted suicides is also considered, this tragedy is magnified. While there will be an estimated 5,000 reported adolescent suicides this year, another 250,000 adolescents will attempt suicide.

It is my hope that this book will provide the needed information and understanding about suicide to caregivers, parents, and others in contact with adolescents. An immediate response to this tragedy is urgently needed; we must have the courage to respond.

# ACKNOWLEDGMENTS

My sincere thanks and gratitude go to the following individuals without whose support, guidance, encouragement, and cooperation this book would not have been possible.

A special "thank you" is extended to Doctor Richard E. Nelson, who has guided my career; to Doctor Sherry Borgers for her support and encouragement; and to Doctor Charles Neuringer, my friend and mentor, who encouraged me to write this book and whose guidance and glowing foreword are deeply appreciated.

To my typist, Mrs. Linda Schopper, who so kindly typed and retyped my manuscript.

To Mr. Harold Gersh for acting as my encouraging grammatical critic and Doctor Mary Gersh for her support and friendship.

To Dean Gilbert Dyck, my long-time friend, for his support and friendship.

To my friend Linda Denniston for her support, assistance, and friendship.

To my friend the Reverend Jerry Spencer for his support, assistance, friendship, and prayers.

To my parents, Florence and Maloy Quinn, for their love, prayers, support, and understanding.

To my other family members, Mike, Jackie, Mary, Jim, Tillie, Esther, Everett, Willis, and Lynne, for their love and support.

To my nieces and nephews, Adam, Ashley, Jennifer, and John, for the joy they have brought to my life.

And to all of my friends and the Regents Center staff for their support and encouragement.

# CONTENTS

# SUICIDAL
# ADOLESCENTS

CHAPTER 1

# THE HISTORY OF SOCIAL ATTITUDES
# TOWARD SUICIDE

ALTHOUGH the first suicide undoubtedly occurred before man began keeping written records, the first known document about suicide was recorded nearly 4,000 years ago. This Egyptian document, known by several titles, such as "The Dispute of a Man with His Soul," "The Dialogue of a Misanthrope with His Soul," or "The Suicide," is dated sometime between 2000 and 1900 years B.C. (Hatton, Valente, and Rink, 1977).

Because parts of this highly literary work are missing and damaged, the text has been interpreted in a variety of ways. One interpretation describes a man tired of life who tries to convince his soul to accompany him to death. His soul is afraid that committing suicide will prohibit the man from a blissful afterlife. Other Egyptologists believe, however, that suicide is not a part of the text and that the literary work only concerns two aspects of death (Hatton et al., 1977).

A review of the history of suicide reveals a broad range of attitudes over the years and within societies, ranging from complete condemnation to viewing suicide as an act that was honorable and brought the individual's family social distinction.

A historical examination of the attitudes of primitive people toward suicide reveals that suicide was looked upon in some cultures as a matter of course and was neither praised nor blamed. In other societies, suicide was highly censured; in yet other societies, suicide was considered courageous and honorable.

3

In many of the early tribes, suicide was part of a ritual or ceremony connected with the major events of the tribe. For example, some primitive people believed that the next world was a continuation of the activities of this world. When a tribal chieftain died, a warrior might kill himself because he believed that the chieftain would need his services in the spirit world just as he had in this world (Dublin, 1963).

The motivations for the suicide of primitive people were, in many instances, similar to those of individuals who commit suicide today. The reasons included the following: "Revenge, a desire for reunion with a departed loved one, escape from pain or punishment or dishonor, a search for immortality" (Dublin, 1963, p. 91).

In the Orient, a custom known as *suttee* existed, where the suicide of a widow was more or less forced upon her at the death of her husband. At first, the rite was mandatory. Later it became a matter of free will. It was believed that a wife could make up for the sins of her husband, relieve him of punishment, and gain him admittance to paradise by committing suttee. The custom continued in parts of India into the nineteenth century until 1828, when legislation was passed to prohibit it (Dublin, 1963).

In Japan, suicide has been accepted even more than in China and India. A custom known as *hara-kiri* (self-disembowelment) was widely practiced by the Samurai, the nobility, and the military class (Dublin, 1963). Sometimes hara-kiri was compulsory; at other times it was done voluntarily. Compulsory hara-kiri allowed an offender of the noble rank to escape being executed like a common criminal. The act generally involved an elaborate ceremony and was considered a very standard routine. Among reasons for voluntary hara-kiri were to protest the policies or crimes of a chief or ruler or to follow the lord and master into the next world (Dublin, 1963).

Voluntary hara-kiri survived until the end of World War II, when it took the form of mass suicide by the Kamikazes. It was estimated that, by the end of World War II, 5,000 young Japanese airmen had committed suicide in Kamikaze missions (Dublin, 1963).

While suicide was considered a noble act in the Orient, other countries and religions have viewed suicide in a more negative way. For example, Judaism has always frowned on suicide. The incidence of suicide among members of the Jewish faith has been very low throughout most of history despite the tremendous persecution and hardships that they have endured since the Temple in Jerusalem was destroyed in A.D. 70 (Dublin, 1963).

There are some instances in history, however, of mass suicide among Jews when persecution reached hideous levels. The first recorded instance of mass suicide was at Masada in A.D. 73. The Zealots, Jewish patriots who resisted the occupation of Judea by the Romans, became entrenched at the fortress at Masada until A.D. 73, when it became apparent that the Roman troops were going to conquer the Zealots at the fortress. The Zealots' leader, Eleazar ben Jair, urged his 960 followers to commit suicide rather than be captured, fearing the men would be killed, the women attacked, and the children sold for slaves. The 960 men, women, and children carried out his wishes and committed mass suicide.

The most recent instance of mass suicide by those of the Jewish faith occurred during Hitler's extermination program (Dublin, 1963).

The strong system of social organization of the Jewish faith is also believed to have a strong impact on the incidence of suicide among members of that faith, as is also the case with members of the Catholic faith (Dublin, 1963).

In ancient Greek history and in the writings of Homer, suicide was viewed with admiration. The earliest suicide mentioned in Greek literature was that of Oedipus' mother, Jocasta, who was considered praiseworthy when she hanged herself after learning that she had been living with her son, the person who had murdered her husband (Alvarez, 1972; Hatton et al., 1977). The Greeks considered her act an honorable way out of an intolerable situation. Homer regarded suicide as a natural and appropriate act, which was usually heroic (Alvarez, 1972; Hatton et al., 1977).

The Greek attitude changed, however, and eventually suicide was viewed as a political offense against the state because it deprived the community of a useful member. Several Greek philosophers opposed suicide: Pythagoras (582-507 B.C.) opposed suicide on the ground that man had no right to leave the world without God's permission; Socrates (469-399 B.C.) supported Pythagoras' viewpoint but felt in some circumstances it should be permissible; Plato (428-347 B.C.) was opposed to suicide except when suicide was ordered by the state and in "extreme cases of poverty, sorrow, or disgrace" (Hatton et al., 1977, p. 3); Aristotle (384-322 B.C.) believed suicide was a cowardly act and considered suicide a crime, as it was a neglect of civic duty (Hatton et al., 1977).

Although the earlier Greek philosophers opposed suicide, the later Greek and Roman philosophers took a more lenient attitude toward suicide. Included in this group were the Cynics, the Cyrenaics, the Stoics, and the Epicureans. An example of this more lenient attitude was demonstrated by the Stoics. The proud, self-reliant, unbending nature of the Stoics was believed to have been sustained only because they considered suicide a rational refuge from extreme suffering and despair (Dublin, 1963). Due deliberation was expected, however, before the act of suicide was accepted.

Though suicide continued through the first and second century with surprising frequency, the position of the Catholic Church from the time of St. Augustine changed that situation dramatically (Dublin, 1963). It was in the fifth century that St. Augustine (A.D. 354-430) spoke out against suicide, stating it was homicide and violated the Sixth Commandment, "Thou shalt not kill." Although he invoked a divine condemnation of suicide, he nevertheless did not consider it should be punishable.

It was not until the second Council of Braga, in A.D. 563, that suicide was formally condemned by the Catholic Church, and it was declared that those who committed suicide would be denied religious funeral rites and burial on consecrated grounds (Alvarez, 1972; Dublin, 1963; Hatton et al., 1977).

During the Middle Ages, when the authority of the Catholic Church was at its peak, the incidence of suicide declined significantly. The influence of the Church remained basically unchanged from the sixth to the sixteenth century. As Hatton et al. (1977) stated, "Change had come with the Reformation and the rediscovery of Classical learning" (p. 5). Philosophers considered the significance of suicide and their writings on the topic both influenced and reflected the attitudes of that time.

The individuals who were influential included Sir Thomas More

(1478-1535), who, in his *Utopia*, suggested an "unprejudiced attitude to suicide" (Hatton et al., 1977, p. 5). John Donne (1573-1631) was one of the Protestant supporters of suicide, who, in *Biathanatos*, published by his son after his death, attacked the attitude of the Church and concluded that suicide was not a violation of the law nor against reason. David Hume (1711-1776), an English philosopher, noted in his *Essay on Suicide* that the Bible does not forbid suicide. He interpreted the Sixth Commandment, "Thou shalt not kill," to forbid killing others and believed man had the right to choose to kill himself. He did, however, believe that those who chose to kill themselves were somewhat mentally unstable or they would not have violated the basic drive of self-preservation. Immanuel Kant (1724-1804), a German philosopher, rejected suicide, as he believed that human life was sacred and that suicide was inconsistent with reason.

During the eighteenth century in France, Montaigne, Voltaire, and Rousseau, three French intellectuals, criticized the hostility toward suicide and the dishonor of the bodies of suicides. Arthur Schopenhauer (1788-1860), another highly respected nineteenth century German philosopher, expressed the view that suicide was "a futile and foolish act" (Hatton et al., 1977, p. 6).

At the close of the nineteenth century, the attitude of William James (1842-1910), an American philosopher, best represented the prevailing attitude toward suicide. James believed that religion was the most powerful deterrent against suicide, but considered suicide a matter of individual choice (Dublin, 1963; Hatton et al., 1977).

A range of attitudes toward suicide currently exists in American society. The Catholic Church still theoretically denies a person who culpably commits suicide the right to a Christian burial. A sensitive pastoral approach, however, would give the deceased the benefit of the doubt regarding freedom of choice and volition and grant burial, which is often a great consolation to the family.

Judaism still frowns on suicide and no branch of Judaism views suicide as an acceptable attitude toward life. Nevertheless, throughout the ages, Jews have recognized that some people will attempt suicide and have thus determined to rule a death a suicide only when it can be proven without a doubt that the person had no reason to despair of life.

In stark contrast, a "276-page book entitled *Suicide Mode D'Emploi (Suicide Operating Instructions)* contains 50 recipes for lethal 'cocktails' that guarantee a 'gentle' death" has been published in France ("French Guide," *The Kansas City Star*, 1982). As of this writing, the article reports that publishing houses in the United States are negotiating for the rights.

Although suicide has been studied for many years, it was not until the late 1950s that suicidology became the subject of intense scientific study. In 1958, the Los Angeles Suicide Prevention Center, funded by a grant from the National Institute of Mental Health, was opened under the direction of two psychologists, Edwin S. Shneidman and Norman L. Farberow. Since that time, numerous other suicide prevention centers have opened across the country.

The relative recency of concerted suicide study is reflected in the fact that the first national conference on suicidology was held in 1968, after which the American Association of Suicidology was formed.

# CHAPTER 2

# ADOLESCENCE AND SUICIDE—
# AN OVERVIEW

WHILE adolescence is often referred to as the "time in life when you have all the fun," in reality, adolescence is not that at all. "Adolescence is a period of rapid growth and development, physical, mental, and psychosocial. It is a critical period associated with many emotional and social conflicts, tensions, pressures, stresses, and home and school difficulties" (Jacobziner, 1960, p. 523).

During this stage of development, the adolescent is trying to become independent while worrying at the same time about the responsibilities that come with independence. Another problem confronting adolescents is that of dealing with peers and adults, for they have two different sets of rules by which to live (Jacobziner, 1960). Thus, the behavior of adolescents often appears inconsistent and contradictory.

There are certain developmental tasks and problems associated with each stage of life development. Schonfeld (1967) stated the three major preoccupations of adolescents are "gaining recognition and prestige, matters associated with sex, and acquiring independence" (p. 1985). Erik Erikson described the task of adolescence as that of establishing a sense of personal identity (Rice, 1981). Adolescents who established a positive self-identity reportedly "had developed a sense of being all right, of being one's self" (LaVoie, 1976, p. 381).

Adolescence is frequently a very stressful period for parents and

adolescents. Behavior problems with adolescents are not at all un-
common. There are primarily five means other than suicide by
which an adolescent may choose to cope with the problems experienced during adolescence. Those five ways are "physical aggression, rebellion, withdrawal (a distinct lack of affect), physical
separation from the problem (going to one's room, running away
from home) or by internalizing the problem where it manifests itself
in the form of psychosomatic illness" (Teicher and Jacobs, 1966, p.
1254). Theories as to why some adolescents choose suicide over the
other five alternatives will be discussed in the section on the motivation underlying suicidal behavior and the etiology of suicidal behavior. Before reviewing the literature on the different theories of
suicide, however, the incidence of committed and attempted suicide
by adolescents and related factors will be discussed.

In 1979, 1,788 adolescents between the ages of fifteen and nineteen and 3,458 adolescents between the ages of twenty and twenty-
four reportedly committed suicide in the United States, making
suicide the second highest cause of death for persons in these age
groups. Together, more than 5,200 adolescents died from self-
inflicted injuries during 1979, accounting for approximately 20 percent of all reported suicides. The rates per 100,000 population were
13.7 for males and 3.3 for females between the ages of fifteen and
nineteen and 27.2 for males and 6.5 for females between the ages of
twenty and twenty-four (*Vital Statistics of the United States*, 1979).

The committed suicide rate varies between racial groups of the
same sex. In 1979, of the total number of reported suicides by white
and black adolescent males, white males were responsible for approximately 90 percent of the committed suicides while black males
were responsible for 10 percent. During that same year, of the total
number of reported suicides by white and black adolescent females,
white females were responsible for 90 percent of the committed
suicides while black females were responsible for 10 percent. Of the
total number of committed suicides by white and black adolescents
during 1979, males of both races were responsible for 80 percent of
the committed suicides while females of both races were responsible
for 20 percent of the committed suicides (*Vital Statistics of the United
States*, 1979).

These statistics on suicide are considered to be understated.

While accidents are the leading cause of death in children and adolescents, there is no way to determine how many of these "accidents" are actually unreported suicides (Miller, 1975). It is generally recognized that the reported number of committed suicides does not reflect the actual number of committed suicides primarily because of the social stigma attached to suicide (Mishara, 1975). Because of the shame experienced by friends and relatives, underreporting occurs (Faigel, 1966). Miller (1975) stated that investigators agree that, because of social, religious, and legal taboos, many committed suicides go unreported. Klagsbrun (1976) stated that "many suicides are hidden by families and reported as accidents or even murders" (p. 16). "Intentionally or unintentionally, many suicidal deaths are never counted" (Mishara, 1975, p. 32). The physician certifying the death may choose to submit the cause of death "by one's own hand as 'accidental' or 'natural' " to help protect the feelings of the victim's family (Mishara, 1975).

In addition, many suicides are not properly diagnosed as suicides. Shneidman and Farberow (1957) found in a ten-year study that suicide notes were left in only 12 to 15 percent of the cases, leading people frequently to conclude that the death was not self-inflicted. All of these factors support the thesis that many committed suicides go unreported, and Litman, Curphey, Shneidman, Farberow, and Tabachnick (1963) stated that "at times we encountered evasion, denial, concealment, and even direct suppression of evidence" (such as relatives deliberately destroying suicide notes) when investigating suicidal deaths (p. 927).

Toolan (1968, 1975) stated that even more committed suicides go unreported for children and adolescents than for adults. Understandably, it is very difficult for parents to deal with their child's suicide, for in doing so, they must face their own role in their child's problems. Bakwin (1957) stated that "ordinarily every effort is made to conceal a suicide death and to attribute it to accident or other cause" (p. 749). The number of unreported committed suicides due to parents' inability to deal with their own feelings and responsibility for what has happened may run as high as 50 percent (Bakwin, 1973). The Los Angeles Suicide Prevention Center has also suggested that 50 percent or more of all suicides are disguised or not reported (Schrut, 1964).

A number of studies have addressed the timing of committed suicides. Powers (1954a, 1956) found that most committed suicides take place in the early morning, although Bergstrand and Otto (1962) found "the majority occurred in the late afternoon or during the night before 12 p.m." (pp. 17-18). Klagsbrun (1976) also reported that the majority of committed suicides occurred in the afternoon between 3 PM and 6 PM. Regarding prevalent days of the week, Powers (1954a, 1956) found that Monday and Tuesday were the days of the week when the majority of committed suicides took place. Bergstrand and Otto (1962) reported November as the month in which the greatest number of suicides occurred. However, by others, the months with the highest incidence of committed suicides were reported to be April through June (Jacobziner, 1965a; Klagsbrun, 1976; Powers, 1954a, 1956). The suicide rate then declines over the summer and fall with the lowest point in December, after which it rises gradually. The three months (April, May, and June) with the highest incidence are the times when many students are concerned about exams and passing into the next grade. Rook (1959) found in a study of Cambridge University students that more than half of the committed suicides occurred around the examination period. Seiden (1966), however, reported that while most believe the majority of student suicides occur around examination time, he found the peak danger period for student suicides to be during the first six weeks of the semester.

While the number of committed suicides by both white and nonwhite adolescents is alarming, the problem magnifies when the number of attempted suicides is considered. Adolescents are responsible for 12 percent of all suicide attempts in the United States (Balser and Masterson, 1959; Corder, Shorr, and Corder, 1974). Estimates of the ratio of attempted suicides to committed suicides have been as high as 120:1 by Rosenkrantz (1978) (although he stated conservative estimates to be as low as 20:1) to 50:1 by Trautman (1966) and Peck (1981).

The rate of attempted and committed suicides differs for males and females. Balser and Masterson (1959) reported that for ages fifteen to nineteen, the female-male ratio of attempted suicides to committed suicides is 10:1, "the highest for any age group" (p. 402). Although adolescent females are responsible for between 75 percent

(Jacobziner, 1960, 1965a, 1965b) and 90 percent (Babow and Kridle, 1972; Bakwin, 1973) of the attempted suicides, as stated earlier, adolescent males are responsible for approximately 80 percent of all adolescent committed suicides (*Vital Statistics of the United States*, 1979).

Males have traditionally chosen more lethal methods for suicide, such as jumping from heights, hanging, firearms, or auto accidents — a factor that no doubt contributes to their higher committed suicide rate. Females, on the other hand, have traditionally chosen more passive and less lethal methods, such as taking pills or wrist slashing, which allows for greater chance of rescue (Bakwin, 1973; Bergstrand and Otto, 1962; Hersh, 1975; Holinger, 1978).

However, a review of the methods chosen by adolescents for suicide during 1979 revealed that females are now using more lethal methods for self-destruction than they have traditionally. The following methods, in order of frequency, were most often chosen by the adolescent females who reportedly committed suicide during 1979: (1) shotgun, hunting rifle, military firearm, and other unspecified firearm, (2) poisoning by solid or liquid substances (includes analgesics, barbiturates, sedatives, tranquilizers, and other drugs), and (3) hanging, strangulation, and suffocation for those between the ages of fifteen and nineteen and handgun, unspecified firearms, and explosives for those between the ages of twenty and twenty-four. The methods most frequently chosen by adolescent males during 1979 were (1) shotgun, hunting rifle, military firearms, and other unspecified firearm, (2) hanging, strangulation, and suffocation, and (3) handgun for those between the ages of fifteen and nineteen and other and unspecified firearm and explosives for those between the ages of twenty and twenty-four.

Repeated attempts using the same method are common. Teicher and Jacobs (1966) found that two-thirds, and Shneidman and Farberow (1957) found that three-fourths, of the victims who committed suicide previously theatened or attempted to take their own lives. In a study of the methods used, Barter, Swaback, and Todd (1968) found that, of forty-five individuals, twenty-seven had made from one to three earlier attempts and four had made more than four attempts using generally the same method each time.

Holinger (1978) found the suicide rates to be the highest for those ages fifteen to nineteen in the Pacific and Mountain divisions and the lowest rates were in the Middle Atlantic and East South Central divisons. For those in the twenty to twenty-four age group, suicide rates were the highest in the Mountain and Pacific divisions and lowest in the Middle Atlantic division. Bakwin (1973) suggested that the different life-styles and the emphasis on play in Las Vegas, Sacramento, and San Francisco are possible reasons for the higher rates in the Western divisions. However, Bakwin (1973) pointed out that the way the statistics were collected could be a contributing factor.

The stage of adolescence is a very critical period and a very difficult stage of development. The major task to be achieved is establishing a sense of personal identity.

The difficulty of adolescence is reflected in the statistics on the number of attempted and committed suicides by adolescents. As stated earlier in this chapter, while the statistics are alarming, it is recognized that the problem is even more tragic than the statistics indicate because of underreporting.

During this stage, adolescents encounter many problems and, of course, suicide always presents one option available for dealing with their problems. From the statistics presented in this chapter, it is clear that many adolescents choose suicide as their way of dealing with problems. The tragedy is that many of these adolescents fail to realize that there are other options available for dealing with problems. These adolescents suffer from tunnel vision; they fail to see other options. They also fail to realize suicide offers a permanent solution to what may otherwise be only a temporary problem.

The statistics presented in this paper indicate that while adolescent males are responsible for a much higher percentage of the committed suicides (80 percent), females are responsible for a much higher percentage of the attempted suicides (between 75 and 95 percent). One reason for this difference is the fact that males have traditionally used more lethal methods in their attempts. Also, it is socially more acceptable for females to ask for help when they have problems and females tend to act more impulsively; thus their attempts are not as well planned and therefore are not as successful, and although females attempt suicide much more often than males, they frequently have less desire to die.

# CHAPTER 3

# THE MOTIVATION UNDERLYING
# SUICIDAL BEHAVIOR

THE first step toward successful diagnosis and treatment of suicidal behavior must obviously be an understanding of the motivation underlying the behavior. While it is common belief that the difference between committed suicide and attempted suicide is simply a matter of success in the suicidal act, many investigators believe there are some specific differences between people who fall within these two groups.

Shneidman (1981) reported that Erwin Stengel has suggested that these two groups are different but with some commonality. It is helpful to think of these two groups as overlapping populations: (1) those who attempt suicide, a few of whom go on to commit suicide and (2) those who commit suicide (this group includes many of whom have previously attempted suicide) (Shneidman, 1981). Stengel (1965) stated only a small portion (10 percent) of the individuals who attempt suicide later commit suicide and that many who do commit suicide are successful on their first attempt.

An important reason for distinguishing these two populations is that those who survive attempted suicide offer a chance to be helped, and there are many more who attempt suicide than commit suicide (Seiden, 1969).

Farberow (1968) stated that motivation underlying suicidal behavior can be either of an interpersonal nature or of an intrapersonal nature. If the motivation is interpersonal, "the suicidal behavior can thus be seen as a means to influence, persuade, force, manipulate, stimulate, change, dominate, reinstate, etc., feelings or behavior in someone else" (p. 392).

If, on the other hand, the motivation is intrapersonal, "the individual's action seems aimed primarily at expressing the pressures and stresses from within and at fulfilling important needs in himself" (Farberow, 1968, p. 392). Farberow (1968) also stated that suicidal behavior of an interpersonal nature is most often found in young and middle-aged individuals while suicidal behavior of an intrapersonal nature is more frequently found in an individual older than sixty who may have suffered a recent loss, who is in ill health, or whose children have left home; so the victim now leads a separate life from the children.

Schuyler (1973) stated that suicidal motivation has two components. The first component is *death seeking*, to escape what is believed to be an unbearable life situation. The second is *instrumental*, an attempt to influence another person's behavior. This second component is frequently described as *manipulative*.

Powers (1956) suggested that attempted suicide is an effort to convey a message to someone about the individual's needs and life circumstances.

Miller (1975) reported that because suicide attempts are disproportionately higher than committed suicides, it is apparent that individuals are seeking to call attention to themselves.

Peck (1968) concurred that attention seeking and manipulation are often present in suicidal behavior. He stated that frequently a trivial reason ascribed by an adolescent for a suicide attempt is not the real cause; through displacement the adolescent has substituted the trivial cause for the real cause. A second function of suicidal behavior, therefore, is to focus attention on a major problem that is manifesting itself through a minor problem by displacement. For example, an adolescent female may attempt suicide by swallowing a handful of aspirin. She may state that she attempted suicide because her parents would not allow her to go away for the weekend with friends. However, further investigation may reveal the real reason for her despondency is the trauma she has experienced from her father's job transfer one year earlier. That transfer meant leaving the school where she was a cheerleader and had many friends. In her new school, she has found it difficult to adjust and make new friends. She no longer perceives herself as the popular cheerleader type she formerly was; thus the depression that culminated in the suicide attempt.

A third function of suicidal behavior, Peck stated, is to communicate to significant others how unhappy the adolescent feels and how much help is needed.

Many who attempt suicide have no intention of dying. In such cases, the suicide attempt is a "cry for help" and a plea to be noticed. "Usually this desperate cry for help comes only after quieter calls and less dramatic messages have brought no results" (Klagsbrun, 1976, p. 25). Frequently, the method chosen for the attempt allows for the greatest chance to be saved. However, sometimes these attempts are accidentally successful. If a nonlethal suicide attempt goes unheeded and is regarded as either nonlethal, attention seeking, or manipulative, it is often repeated in a more serious way. Schuyler (1973) stated that unanswered cries for help frequently result in suicidal death.

Jacobziner (1965a) found that in 52 percent of the attempts, either one or both parents were present at the time of the attempt, 5 percent of the time an adult relative or friend was present, and in only 38 percent of the cases was the adolescent home alone. These statistics lend support to the theory that suicidal behavior is frequently a means of communicating a message. Additionally, as discussed earlier, most committed suicides took place during the hours of the day when others were around to rescue them. The committed suicides did not take place during the time when others were normally sleeping.

Jacobziner (1965a, 1965b) stated that every suicide attempt or threat must be taken seriously and the individuals should be promptly referred for treatment. Unfortunately, since adolescence is a time when emotions frequently change, attempted suicide or serious talk of suicide is often brushed off lightly.

Research has shown that adolescents who committed suicide had difficulty communicating with others before their suicide (Hatton et al., 1977). Also, adolescents who committed suicide were generally more isolated, felt more hopeless, and were less likely to give out signals for help than those who did not commit suicide (Hatton et al., 1977). Adolescent males are generally less communicative by nature. Hatton et al. (1977) suggest this may explain why more males commit suicide although three times as many females attempt suicides.

In contrast to the adolescent male who commits suicide, the adolescent female is more likely to signal for help by threatening or attempting suicide (Hatton et al., 1977). This behavior is considered to be consistent with the fact that it is more socially acceptable for females to ask for medical help and to communicate their fears and anxieties to those around them. Hatton et al. (1977) did point out, however, that by the time someone commits suicide, there is usually no one with whom the person feels communication is possible.

In research conducted by the Los Angeles Suicide Prevention Center, some specific differences were found between the committed suicide group and the other groups of suicidal adolescents studied. Those who committed suicide had a history of more frequent psychiatric hospitalization combined with more emotional disturbance and fewer previous suicide attempts (Hatton et al., 1977). The research also indicated that the adolescent who commits suicide has more of a disposition toward self-destruction and thus requires less overt stress than peers to trigger the suicide act (Hatton et al., 1977).

Thus, it appears that it is inaccurate to say that it is only a matter of success in the suicidal act that differentiates those who commit suicide from those who attempt suicide.

The reviewed research in this chapter indicates that those who committed suicide differed from those who attempted suicide in the following ways: (1) They were more isolated, (2) they felt more hopeless about the future, (3) they were less likely to give out signals for help, (4) they had a history of more frequent psychiatric hospitalization, (5) they were more emotionally disturbed, (6) they had fewer previous suicide attempts, and (7) they had more of a disposition toward self-destruction.

# CHAPTER 4

# THE ETIOLOGY OF SUICIDAL BEHAVIOR

## FAMILIAL TENDENCIES

REFERENCES to families who have a history of suicidal behavior frequently occur in the reviewed literature. In a study of a family of four generations in which seven members committed suicide and one member made several attempts, Shapiro (1935) suggested "that suicidal tendencies as such are not directly inherited as a unit factor, but appear as part of susceptibility to mental disease which may be inherited" (p. 553).

Swanson (1960) in a study of one set of identical twins found that one twin committed suicide within a few months of an earlier attempt by the other. The second twin was not aware of the suicide attempt by the first twin; he had only been told that the first twin had suffered another nervous breakdown.

Specific studies on genetic influence were conducted by Kallmann and Anastasio (1946) and by Kallmann, De Porte, De Porte, and Feingold (1949). The researchers in both studies believed that if heredity was a major determining factor in suicidal behavior, then by studying twins they should be able to find evidence to support that thesis. More specifically, they felt they would find a concordant tendency to suicide more frequently in monozygotic (one-egg) than in dizygotic (two-egg) twins, despite differences in their environment, if heredity is a major contributing factor.

In the first study, eleven sets of twins were studied and in the second study twenty-seven sets of twins were studied. Both studies included monozygotic and dizygotic twins.

19

The conclusion drawn in each study was that suicide does not generally occur in both twins, even if they have the same type of personality or the same type of mental disorder. They believe the reason for this discordant behavior is that suicide is a result of a combination of many complex factors and that duplication of such factors is highly unlikely, even in identical twins who might have the same type of mental disorder and comparable social backgrounds.

Kallmann et al. (1949) pointed out that these studies tend to disprove the popular belief that the tendency to commit suicide reappears in some families as the result of a heredity trait or a genetically transmitted personality deviation.

In a study of a group of adolescents who had attempted suicide, Teicher and Jacobs (1966) found that in 44 percent of the cases, there had been a successful suicide or suicide attempt by one or more close friends or relatives and in 25 percent of the cases, there had been a suicide attempt by the mother or father of the adolescent.

Tishler, McKenry, and Morgan (1981) stated that in a study of 108 adolescent suicide attempters, 22 percent reported that at least one family member had previously exhibited suicidal behavior.

While the heredity studies indicate that a tendency to suicidal behavior is not genetic, the research by Teicher and Jacobs (1966) and Tishler et al. (1981) may explain why it appears to be genetically transmitted. Teicher and Jacobs (1966) suggested a suicide or suicide attempt by a parent or significant other person in the adolescent's life may serve as a role model for the adolescent and demonstrate a possible solution to problems that may not otherwise have been considered.

These studies do not support the common belief that suicide "runs in families." Rather, a more likely reason that attempted suicides and committed suicides are found in multiples in some families, while in other families there are no instances of suicidal behavior, is that in the first instance, suicidal behavior by a parent or significant other person has served as a role model and a possible alternative solution to life's problems.

Victoroff (1977) reported that studies indicate that individuals whose families have had a suicide are nine times more likely to commit suicide than those with no history of suicide in the family. These statistics add credence to the concept of modeling suicidal behavior.

With this information in mind, caregivers should be alerted to a higher risk of suicidal behavior in adolescents who report a family history of suicidal behavior.

## ADOLESCENCE—A STAGE OF DEVELOPMENT

Statistics indicate that suicide occurs more frequently during adolescence than at any earlier age. The increase in attempted and committed suicides during this stage "has generally been linked to the 'stress and strain' of adolescence, especially to conflicts over sexuality and dependency" (Seiden, 1969, p. 27).

Many changes take place during adolescence. One of the most significant issues confronting adolescents is that of sexual adjustment (Jacobziner, 1960). Gorceix (1963) stated that while the adolescent is sexually mature, this maturity is not accepted by society.

Bigras, Gauthier, Bouchard, and Tasse (1966) in a study of twenty-one adolescent females who had attempted suicide found either a masculine identification or absence of any sexual identification in all of the females. Not one case of true feminine identification was found in the study.

Schneer, Kay, and Brozovsky (1961) in a study involving eighty-four hospitalized adolescents who had threatened or attempted suicide found the females were generally preoccupied with being raped, although they were active socially with males, sometimes even promiscuous. The adolescent males studied were concerned about their masculine identification and genital damage and acted belligerent with their parents, particularly their mother.

Zilboorg (1937) suggested that suicidal behavior in men is related to men's passive homosexual drives. He stated that civilized men have to curb their aggressive instincts unlike primitive races. When men do this, Zilboorg stated, it sometimes arouses threats of passivity and feminity, which in turn triggers a fear of homosexuality, which becomes a motive for suicide.

A number of instances of rather bizarre hangings by adolescent males were found in the literature. In all of these cases, erotic sexual stimulation and satisfaction were sought through self-induced suffocation. In some of these cases, the adolescent males were wearing women's clothing; in others the males were naked. In some instances, the feet and/or hands had been tied together. There was evidence of masturbation in all cases. The intent of these males was orgasm, not death; during the self-strangulation, they unintentionally killed themselves.

Since it was known that some of these males had previously engaged in this act, researchers have concluded that these deaths are accidental and not intentional suicides. References to this "hanging syndrome" activity were made in the literature by Bakwin, 1973; Ford, 1957; Litman et al., 1963; Neuringer, 1975; Schechter, 1957; Shankel and Carr, 1956; and Stearns, 1953.

Problems with sexual adjustment and identification were present in all studies reviewed in this section. These studies are representative of the potential problems facing adolescents when they have problems with sexual adjustment and identification. Sexuality obviously carries with it a great deal of emotional turmoil for adolescents. In our society today, much emphasis is placed on sexuality, which no doubt accentuates this problem for adolescents.

## MENTAL DISORDERS

Seiden (1969) stated that depression and schizophrenia are two mental disorders frequently linked to suicide. While some individuals who attempt or commit suicide are depressed, it is important to note that depression is not a prerequisite for suicidal behavior.

Depression in adolescence is frequently associated with some loss of a love object. This loss may be through separation or death (Seiden, 1969).

Faigel (1966) stated that depression associated with the loneliness experienced from loss through death or separation is the most common underlying problem in suicidal adolescents and children.

Toolan (1962, 1968) said that the common factor in depressive reactions is the loss of a love object. Toolan's (1962) study of a group of children and adolescents who had made suicide threats and attempts indicated that although a large number of the children and adolescents had been diagnosed as having behavior and character disorders, upon closer examination they showed many signs of depression.

However, Balser and Masterson (1959) concluded that depression is not an important factor in the suicidal behavior of adolescents.

Toolan (1962) suggested that suicide attempts by children and adolescents have frequently been overlooked because of the common belief that children and adolescents do not get depressed. He noted that while they do not exhibit the same depressive reactions as do adults, children and adolescents do exhibit other depressive symptoms.

Gould (1965) stated that common depressive symptoms in children and adolescents are "(1) loss of interest in social environment and loss of drive; (2) feelings of sadness and emptiness; (3) eating disturbances (anorexia mostly; bulimia occasionally); (4) sleeping disturbances (insomnia mostly; 'oversleeping' occasionally); (5) hypomotility; and (6) feelings of loneliness" (p. 235). He further stated that depression in children and adolescents is often masked by "temper tantrums, boredom, restlessness, rebelliousness and defiance, somatic and hypochondrial preoccupation, 'accidental' injuries, running away, and delinquent and antisocial acts (these last two being more prevalent in adolescents than in children)" (p. 235).

Faigel (1966) stated that "depression is often characterized by boredom, restlessness, preoccupation with trivia, and acting out by means of dare-devil behavior involving delinquency, alcohol, sex, or drugs" (p. 189).

Tishler et al. (1981) noted that of the suicidal adolescents studied, "a majority of these suicidal adolescents evidenced sleep disturbances, weight change, and inappropriate affect (affect that is incongruent with the situation)" (p. 88).

Miller (1975) stated that sometimes animals and pets become the recipients of an adolescent's affection. And, although the adolescent may sometimes have superficial relationships, the adolescent will not gain any emotional support from the relationships.

Tooley (1978) cited a lack of hope in the future as the factor that distinguishes the suicidally depressed adolescent from other young people who are trying to deal with the problems of identification.

An important observation about depression and suicide is that the danger period for suicide is not during the peak of the depression but is instead during the three-month period following that point (Hyde and Forsyth, 1978; Seiden, 1969; Shneidman and Farberow, 1957). With the draining depression gone, the adolescent may have the energy to commit the act.

The second mental disorder connected with suicidal behavior is that of schizophrenia. Toolan (1962) found that response to auditory hallucinatory commands frequently triggered serious suicide attempts.

Balser and Masterson (1959) found that of thirty-seven adolescent suicide attempters, twenty-nine had been diagnosed as schizophrenic. "Specific pathology included dissociation, hallucinations, delusional ideas, withdrawal, suspiciousness, and lack of communicability" (Balser and Masterson, 1959, p. 404). These researchers concluded that there is a closer relationship between schizophrenic reactions and suicidal tendencies in adolescents than between suicidal tendencies and depression.

It can be concluded, therefore, that while suicidal behavior may result from depression, an adolescent need not be depressed for suicidal behavior to occur. It was also pointed out that depression in children and adolescents frequently does not evident itself in the same way that it does in the adult population, a fact that has sometimes led individuals to inaccurately believe that depression does not occur in children and adolescents.

Schizophrenia in some cases has led to serious suicide attempts. In such cases, auditory hallucinatory commands have frequently triggered these attempts.

## PERCEPTION OF DEATH

The adolescent's perception of death is a significant factor in the suicidal tendencies of the individual. Some adolescents view death as an appropriate response to their parents' wish for them to die. (This may be either conscious or unconscious, verbal or nonverbal.) If a child becomes expendable, in that the child is no longer needed or can no longer be tolerated, then suicidal behavior often occurs after the adolescent receives such a message (Sabbath, 1969). An example of such a situation is the juvenile delinquent. The adolescent may no longer be an object of affection or may no longer meet the parents' needs.

Lester (1967) found that those studied who had attempted suicide or threatened suicide feared death less than those who had never considered suicide. He also found that those who had attempted or threatened suicide were more concerned with the manipulative aspects of death.

An adolescent's view of death can be assumed to be an influential factor on the individual's subsequent behavior. While some adolescents may view death as an appropriate response to a parental message, other adolescents view suicidal behavior as a manipulative act; still others view suicide as the only possible solution to their problems.

## AGGRESSION

Stengel (1965) suggested that aggression toward others, not oneself, is a characteristic of a person who attempts suicide. He stated that this is the distinguishing factor between the person who attempts suicide and the person who commits suicide. Moss and Hamilton (1956) stated there are three coexisting (unconscious or partially conscious) determinants of suicide and one of them was "hostility or rage directed toward important persons upon whom blame was placed for present frustrations, which because of guilt, fear, or anxiety became self-directed" (p. 814).

Aggression turned inward, therefore, is considered a characteristic of an adolescent who commits suicide.

## IMPULSIVENESS

Impulsiveness is another common cause of suicide attempts. Zilboorg (1937) stated his impression that young people commit suicide with more impulsiveness and fewer rational reasons than those of the adult population.

Jacobziner (1960, 1965a, 1965b) suggested that the much higher incidence in suicide attempts by adolescent females, as compared to adolescent males, is due to their greater impulsiveness; their actions are impulsive, not premeditated, with no intent to die. The attempt is simply a sudden reaction to some stressful situation.

Bergstrand and Otto (1962) found in their study of Swedish children and adolescents that females act more impulsively than adolescent males and that the reasons for the attempts were frequently rather insignificant, such as love conflicts.

Gould (1965) pointed out that although impulsiveness leads to many suicide attempts, such hasty and poorly planned attempts have less chance of being successful.

The research reviewed supports the theory that impulsiveness is frequently responsible for suicide attempts in adolescent females. This same conclusion is also supported by the earlier reported data, which indicated that while adolescent females are responsible for between 75 and 90 percent of the attempted suicides, they are only responsible for 20 percent of the adolescent-committed suicides.

## DRUG ABUSE

Drug abuse and suicide have been cited by Schonfeld (1967) and Trautman (1966) as a means of escaping from intolerable life situations.

Schonfeld (1967) suggested that our affluent society has incorporated in the adolescent the need for every wish to be met immediately, to avoid pain and frustration at any cost, and to be happy all of the time. It is considered acceptable to run away from the problems and frustrations of living. When life's problems get too overwhelming, Schonfeld stated, adolescents escape by turning to drugs, alcohol, withdrawal, or suicide. An increased usage of alcohol and drugs by adolescents as well as increased social isolation are warning signals or prodromal clues to suicidal behavior.

Unfortunately, adolescents turn to drugs and alcohol many times as a means of escape but fail to realize that they offer only a temporary "answer" to their problems. Suicide, on the other hand, offers a permanent solution to what otherwise may have been only a temporary problem.

## SIBLING POSITION

Since adolescents do not experience life in a vacuum but rather as a member of a family, it is important to examine how the family may influence suicidal behavior. Of particular interest with children in families is how their sibling position in the family influences their lives.

Cantor (1972) found in a study of ten firstborn female suicide attempters that seven had brothers as their next younger sibling.

Toolan (1962) found in his study of 102 suicide attempters that forty-nine were firstborn children. He feels this large percentage may reflect a tendency of first children to feel unloved and rejected following the birth of a sibling.

Kallmann et al. (1949) in their study of twins and only children found that only children are neither more nor less likely to commit suicide than other children in the general population or twins.

Thus, it would appear from these research studies that in the case of firstborn children with younger siblings, the sibling position may be a contributing factor to suicidal behavior. However, the likelihood of an only child committing suicide is neither more nor less than other children or twins, the research indicates.

## FAMILY PROBLEMS AND LOSS OF A LOVED ONE

A second family-related issue is how suicidal behavior may be influenced by broken homes and disorganized families. Stengel (1965) pointed out that one problem with this issue is that there is no clear-cut definition of a broken home. Investigators use the term throughout the literature; however, there is no uniform definition. To some it means there is at least one parent lacking and to others it is used more broadly to include all forms of family disorganization, such as conflict in the family and disharmony between parents.

The influence of broken homes and family disorganization has been studied by investigators in countries outside of the United

States. Bigras et al. (1966) in a study of the families of twenty-one adolescent suicide attempters in Canada found that eleven of the families appeared to be disorganized. In fifteen out of twenty-one of these families, the father was described as passive, inefficient in his role as a father, or physically absent. In these same families, nine of twenty-one mothers were most often described as cold and rigid.

A study by Glaser (1965) of fifteen children and adolescent suicide attempters in this country found that the father had played a very passive and disinterested role.

Bergstrand and Otto (1962) in a study of adolescent male and female attempters from Swedish families found that 44 percent of the attempters were from broken homes.

In a study of Japanese families, Iga (1981) found a significant difference in families where neither the biological father nor mother was living with the adolescent when he or she was age seventeen. (Iga states that *biological* is important to define here because stepparents in Japan tend to be regarded as outsiders rather than parents, and the relationship between the child and stepparents is expected to be strained.) In 11 percent of the suicidal adolescents, as opposed to 1 percent of the control group, neither the biological father nor mother lived with the adolescent at age seventeen. Thirteen percent of the suicidal adolescents studied came from families where neither the biological father nor mother took care of the children during the summers when they were in grade school; 3 percent of the nonsuicidal adolescents came from such families.

Numerous studies have also been conducted in the families of suicidal adolescents in this country. Cantor (1972) found in a study of seventeen adolescent suicide attempters that ten of the seventeen were from broken homes and it was the father who was absent in all ten instances.

Jacobziner (1965a, 1965b) found that in nearly 22 percent of the cases studied where the adolescents had attempted suicide, the parents were not living together. In 12 percent of these cases, the father was deceased.

Tishler et al. (1981) reported in a study of 108 adolescent suicide attempters that only 49 percent were living with both parents at the time of the suicide attempt and that almost 50 percent of these adolescents reported that at least one of their parents had been divorced while 60 percent assessed their parents' marriage as poor.

Teicher and Jacobs (1966) found in twenty adolescent suicide attempters that the mothers of all fifteen of the males studied had either had illegitimate children or were pregnant at the time of their marriage. Seventy percent of the mothers were separated and 38 percent had been married more than one time.

In another study of families of suicide attempters, Jacobs and Teicher (1967) found 72 percent of those who had attempted suicide, as opposed to 53 percent in the control group, were from broken homes.

Toolan (1962, 1968) found that less than one-third of the adolescents studied who had attempted suicide were living with both parents at the time they were hospitalized.

Barter et al. (1968) reported that of forty-five adolescent suicide attempters studied only twenty-one came from families where the natural parents were living together, and in eleven of those cases there were severe marital problems.

Schneer et al. (1961) in a study of eighty-four suicide attempters (ages twelve to sixteen) found that "the biological father had usually lost more or less permanent contact with the family" (p. 508). The biological mother was usually still in contact although this contact was characterized by gross neglect or was affected by her intermittent illness, by her child's intermittent illness, or by her employment away from home. "The mother was often punitive or detached" (p. 508).

Wenz (1978) found in the families of 194 adolescent suicide attempters that those included in the high risk group were from families where there was "(a) high degree of disorientation from cultural and family norms and (b) feelings of family powerlessness" (pp. 4647).

Greer (1964) reported that the incidence of parental loss was significantly higher among a group of suicidal than nonsuicidal neurotics.

Zilboorg (1937) suggested that if young persons lose an immediate family member (father, mother, brother, or sister) when they are at "the height of their oedipus complex or transition to puberty" (p. 22), there is a real danger of suicide.

Topol and Reznikoff (1982) studied 100 adolescents between the ages of thirteen and nineteen. Their study of thirty hospitalized suicidal adolescents, thirty-four nonsuicidal hospitalized adolescents, and thirty-five nonhospitalized coping adolescents revealed that the hospitalized suicidal adolescents were found not only to have the greatest number of total problems and peer problems but also the most serious family problems. The hospitalized adolescents who had attempted suicide were also found to have a significantly greater degree of hopelessness than the nonsuicidal hospitalized adolescents.

In a study of both attempted and committed suicides, Dorpat, Jackson, and Ripley (1965) found that 50 percent of the committed suicides and 64 percent of the attempted suicides came from broken homes. Divorce was the type of loss most common in the attempted suicide group and death was the most common loss in the committed suicide group.

Paffenbarger and Asnes (1966) in a study of college-age males who had committed suicide found that early loss or the absence of a father was one of the factors differentiating the group who had committed suicide from the control group. "The differentiating familial characteristics included college training of parents, professional status of the father, marital separation of parents, and death of the father" (p. 1036).

Jacobs and Teicher (1967) do not believe it is "the loss of a love object per se that is so distressing but the loss of love, i.e., the reciprocal intimacy, spontaneity, and closeness that one experiences in a 'primary relationship' " (p. 146).

Peck (1968) pointed out that the loss of a love object can assume a number of forms. Not only can the loss result from divorce, separation, death, etc., but it can also result from a form of homesickness experienced by adolescents when separated from the family for the first time, from a breakup between a girlfriend and boyfriend, etc. Teicher and Jacobs (1966) noted that the loss of an older sibling (marriage, armed services, college, etc.) may also have a significant influence on suicidal behavior.

McAnarney (1979) stated that the changes that are taking place in the American family—in particular the loss of the intact family through divorce, separation, or death—are important variables in the backgrounds of adolescents who commit suicide. She said that with sufficient family support most adolescents are able to pass successfully through adolescence without major problems.

However, if the adolescent has lost a parent or both parents and does not have satisfactory parent substitutes, the adolescent may be severely handicapped in trying to complete this stage of development without being vulnerable to impulsive, self-destructive behavior in an effort to avoid dealing with failure (McAnarney, 1979).

Frederick (1976) presented the following profile of a suicidal adolescent male: "A typical profile for the young suicidal male is one in which the father has died or been separated before the boy is 16 years of age. The father is often a successful professional or business man. There has been a characteristic lack of close father-son relationship which brings on feelings of rejection, anxiety, sleeplessness, and heavy smoking" (p. 2).

Frederick continued by also presenting a profile of a suicidal adolescent female. He stated, "By contrast, the young suicidal female is the product of a self-centered mother and an ineffectual father. After feeling rejection by her family and/or boyfriend, she frequently attempts to take her life" (p. 2).

In both instances, the fathers are considered to be very significant figures. Frederick stated that while mothers have been blamed many times for the misbehavior of their children, many emotional problems, particularly with boys, "can be laid squarely at the doorstep of the father" (p. 2).

The disintegration of the family structure is manifested through an increase in suicidal behavior by the adolescent family members. The studies repeatedly evidenced more suicidal behavior in broken families (due to death, divorce, or separation), families where there were severe marital problems, families where the father was passive and ineffective, families where a close relationship between father and son was lacking, and families where the mothers were cold, rigid, punitive, detached, and/or self-centered.

From this research, it appears there is a strong relationship between the breakdown of the American family and the increased number of adolescent suicides. As Peck (1982) stated, "The family seems to be a key element in preventing suicide" (p. 27). He continued by stating, "Loving, concerned parents and relatives are probably the best insurance" (p. 27).

These statements acknowledge the importance of the family and the significance of love, concern, support, and understanding within the family and toward the adolescent. The importance of a loving, caring, understanding, and supportive family cannot be overemphasized.

## SOCIAL ISOLATION

Social isolation is another critical factor that influences suicidal behavior. Stengel (1965) stated that a lack of a secure relationship with parents may have a long-term effect on an individual's ability to establish relationships with others. Such individuals may find themselves in social isolation, which, Stengel stated, is one of the critical causal factors in suicidal behavior.

Barter et al. (1968) studied forty-five adolescent suicide attempters and reported that of those who continue suicidal behavior after hospitalization, "there is an association with the living situation" (p. 527). "The teen-ager who is alienated from his family and who does not or cannot live at home, who has poor peer relationships, and an inadequate social life may be the one for whom the risk of continued suicidal behavior is high" (Barter et al., 1968, p. 527).

Jacobs and Teicher (1967) stated that suicidal adolescents usually have a long history of problems that progressively isolates them. For example, an adolescent female may have many conflicts with her parents that eventually lead to alienation. She may then forgo all other meaningful social relationships for a relationship with a boyfriend. When that relationship breaks up, she finds herself alienated from parents and friends, and a suicide attempt is likely.

Seiden (1966) in a study comparing twenty-three college students who had committed suicide with the total student body found that those in the suicidal group were more withdrawn than those from the total student body. He stated that these students were "uniformly described as terribly shy, virtually friendliness [sic] individuals, alienated from all but the most minimal social interactions" (p. 398).

Bakwin (1973) also reported that social isolation and withdrawal were the personality traits most frequently found in students who committed suicide. These research studies all support the fact that isolation can be a major contributing factor to suicidal behavior.

The research on social isolation strongly supports the importance of social relationships and the danger in the lack of such relationships. Social isolation is repeatedly mentioned as a warning signal or prodromal clue of suicidal behavior throughout the literature.

## ACADEMIA

A number of investigators have studied the incidence of suicide among college students. The first such study was reported by Raphael, Power, and Berridge (1937). Their research conducted at the University of Michigan was prompted by the fact that more than half of the student deaths at that institution had resulted from suicide.

Since that time, a number of other investigators have studied the problem of student suicide. Parnell (1951) in a study of the incidence of suicide during 1947-1949 among students at Oxford University found that the suicide rate for undergraduates was eleven times higher than for the general population of the same age.

Parrish (1957) studied the incidence of suicide among students at Yale University. He found the suicide rate among the general population of white males fifteen to twenty-four years old to be 6.6 per 100,000, while the suicide rate of Yale University students was 9.0 per 100,000. Parrish thus concluded that the suicide rate among Yale University students was not statistically significantly higher than that of the general population of the same age.

Lyman (1961) in a study comparing the suicide rate between students at British universities and the nation in general found that the students at Oxford University had a significantly higher suicide rate. The rates were 26.4 per 100,000 at Oxford, 21.3 at Cambridge University, 16.3 at the University of London, 5.9 at seven other British universities, and 4.1 for the national population of England and Wales (Lyman, 1961).

Braaten and Darling (1962) studied 134 students at Cornell University. Those 134 students did not include any committed suicides but did include four other groups: (1) those who showed no concern with suicide, (2) those who intellectualized concern with suicide (little feeling), (3) those who threatened or were preoccupied with suicide, and (4) those who had attempted suicide. Major results of this study included the finding that more suicidal tendencies were found among undergraduates than among graduate students. The study also showed no significant difference between the number of suicide attempts by women and those by men. Braaten and Darling (1962) also reported that the suicidal group were more depressed and showed more psychopathology than the nonsuicidal group.

Bruyn and Seiden (1965) found in a study involving both students and nonstudents at the University of California, Berkeley, that (1) the suicide rate for students was significantly higher than the suicide rate of a comparable group of nonstudents, (2) the suicide rate for college students was positively correlated with age, as was also the case in the general population, (3) the mortality rate was more favorable for students than for a comparable group of nonstudents, and (4) more studies need to be conducted to determine how the suicide-prone student differs from other students.

Seiden (1966) also reviewed the aforementioned study at the University of California, Berkeley. He reported that the suicidal students differed from the other students "on the variables of age, class standing, major subject, nationality, emotional condition, and academic achievement" (p. 399). He also reported that the suicidal group was older, contained more graduate students, language majors, and foreign students and evidenced more emotional disturbance. The undergraduate students in the suicidal group had done better academically than the other nonsuicidal undergraduates.

Other findings included (1) the peak danger period for suicides was during the first six weeks of the semester; (2) most of the students gave repeated warnings of their suicidal intent and many evidenced prodromal clues; (3) "major precipitating factors were: worry over schoolwork, chronic concerns about physical health (sometimes of a decidedly bizarre nature), and difficulties with interpersonal relationships" (p. 399); and (4) an increase in student suicides was predicted on the basis of the fact that changes are taking place in the ages of students in college.

Seiden (1966) also found that the mean grade point average of the undergraduates who committed suicide was 3.18 while the mean grade point average of the other undergraduates was 2.50. Of those undergraduates who committed suicide, 58 percent had won scholastic awards as opposed to 5 percent of the other undergraduate students. Every undergraduate who committed suicide had lower grades in his or her most recent semester.

Reports from friends and relatives revealed that these students were dissatisfied with their grades and despondent about their academic ability. The graduate students who committed suicide did not show any decline in their most recent semester grades.

As previously mentioned in this book, Paffenbarger and Asnes (1966) found in a study of University of Pennsylvania and Harvard University students who had committed suicide that early loss or the absence of a father differentiated the group who had committed suicide from the control group.

Peck (1968) stated that while there appears to be a higher incidence of suicide at the top-ranked colleges and universities than at other colleges where there is less academic pressure, it is important to note a difference in the ages of these two groups of students. The larger top-ranked colleges and universities typically have more graduate students and the average age is in the late twenties. On the other hand, at the other small colleges, the average age is nineteen.

Since research has repeatedly shown that the incidence of suicide increases with age, it may be the difference in the age groups and not the greater pressure that is responsible for the higher incidence of suicide at the top-ranked colleges and universities.

Research by the Los Angeles Suicide Prevention Center has indicated that the major factor in student suicides is not grades or pressure to succeed but rather "loss or separation from a loved one" (Peck, 1968, p. 113).

Peck and Schrut (1971) studied four groups of college students over a two-year period in Los Angeles County. Included in the four groups were committed suicides, threatened suicides, attempted suicides, and a nonsuicidal control group. Data from this study support the theory that the incidence of suicide is higher at larger colleges and universities than at the small liberal arts and junior colleges.

Peck and Schrut (1971) observed that the factors accounting for the largest variance in these suicides were age and sex ratio. They stated that the higher incidence of older male students (older than twenty-five) may account for the higher incidence of suicide at the larger universities.

Problems in school have been cited by other investigators as causes for suicidal behavior. Teicher and Jacobs (1966) reported that in a group of suicide attempters studied between the ages of fourteen and eighteen, one-third were not enrolled at the time of the suicide attempt. However, none of these adolescents had been dropped from school because of poor grades. Teicher and Jacobs (1966) also stated that when adolescents do not attend school, they lose a very important resource for establishing and maintaining relationships with friends.

Barter et al. (1968) in a study involving forty-five adolescent suicide attempters, all under age twenty-one, found problems in school were reported for thirty-five of the forty-five adolescents. These problems included poor grades, truancy, and disciplinary matters. Frequently, these problems had begun within a year or two of the time the adolescent was hospitalized. Of those in the group who had demonstrated lifelong problems in school, many had dropped out or were considering dropping out at the time of hospitalization.

In another study related to children and adolescents and their suicide attempts, Otto (1965) reported that of the sixty-two adolescents studied (ages twelve to twenty), school problems were cited as the cause of some of the suicide attempts. However, only 6.2 percent of the adolescents and children cited school problems as the reason for the attempt. Otto (1965) pointed out that when the school problems were compared to the other difficulties, they were of relatively slight importance.

Sartore (1976) said that no definite correlation between school failure and suicide exists. However, he believes that failure in school leads to loneliness and that loneliness can trigger the depression that is frequently found in suicide. Sartore (1976) stated that an individual's self-perception, which is influenced by academic performance, is a determinant in suicidal behavior.

Hendin (1975a, 1975b, 1982) reported studies with suicidal students who he believed were "drawn to death as a way of life" (1975a, p. 328). He reported, "These students see their relationships with their parents as dependent on their emotional if not physical death and become tied to their parents in a kind of death knot" (Hendin,

1975a, p. 328).

When the situation changes for such an adolescent, for example, when the adolescent leaves home and goes to college, Hendin believes the adolescent perceives a threat to change the feelings of depression experienced up until that point. Since the adolescent does not know how to live with this change, Hendin has suggested that the adolescent will often opt for suicide in order to hold onto the familiar depression that had previously been experienced.

The fear of being free of the depression, which has defined the adolescent-parental relationship for so long, is so great that the adolescent turns to suicide for a lack of knowing how else to handle this freedom. This, Hendin believes, is the reason for many student suicides.

Contrary to the popular belief that academic pressure is the key factor in student suicides, the reviewed research indicates that (1) as with the general population, there is a positive correlation between the ages of students who commit suicide; (2) grades are sometimes perceived by the student who commits suicide as a problem, but that same student's grades may be considered by others to be respectable; (3) a school setting provides an opportunity to establish and maintain social relationships that can help protect an individual from the danger of social isolation; and (4) loss or separation may be the real key factor responsible for triggering student suicides.

## MEDIA

The influence of the media on suicidal behavior has been studied by Motto (1967). He examined the incidence of suicide in seven cities that had experienced newspaper blackouts, comparing the incidence of suicide during those periods to the mean rate for the five previous years. Motto concluded that reporting of suicides in the newspapers did not precipitate other suicides.

However, Bakwin (1973) noted that there was an increase in the number of adolescent suicides after the suicides of Janis Joplin and Jimi Hendrix, both rock entertainers, who took drug overdoses. She suggested that the increase in suicides was attributable to the extensive press coverage of those suicides.

A song entitled "The Ode to Billy Joe" (Gentry, 1967), about a teenager who committed suicide, was the No. 1 song on the charts for many weeks in 1967 (Seiden, 1969). Although the topic of suicide remains generally taboo, this song became and remained popular for sometime.

While there appear to be conflicting beliefs as to the impact of the media on suicidal behavior, in reality, it seems that the impact of this factor is very difficult to accurately measure.

It is generally accepted that talking about suicide does not implant the idea in an individual's head. However, for those who are suicidal, the self-inflicted death of another individual may serve as a role model. In this way then, the media could be influential in an individual's subsequent suicidal behavior.

## CULTURE

Suicidal behavior is also influenced by cultural factors. Seiden (1969) stated there are three ways in which cultural factors may influence suicidal behavior: (1) by its acute psychological effects, (2) by the acceptability of suicidal behavior in society, and (3) by the other alternative behaviors afforded by society.

Japan exemplifies the cultural influence of suicide. The general attitude toward suicide in Japan was reported by Seiden (1969) to be more acceptable than in many other countries. The suicide rate in Japan for adolescents fifteen to twenty-four years of age was reported by Iga (1981) to be one of the highest in the world. The rate reported in 1973 was 16.5 per 100,000 in Japan while the reported rate in 1973 for the United States was 10.6 (Iga, 1981).

The Japanese are highly status conscious; education is believed to be almost the only way to achieve security (Iga, 1981). Therefore, there is a tremendous emphasis, to the point of obsession, on educational success (Iga, 1981). This tremendous emphasis on educational success is believed to be the key factor responsible for the high suicide rate of adolescents in Japan.

A second example of cultural influence is illustrated in a study by Dizmang, Watson, May and Bopp (1974). They studied over a seven-year period the incidence of suicide among the Shoshone and the Bannock Indians (grouped linguistically as the Shoshonean) who live in Fort Hall, Idaho.

These investigators found the general suicide rate for this population to be ninety-eight per 100,000 and that half of the suicides were by individuals younger than twenty-five (Dizmang et al., 1974).

They reported that with the relocation of these Indians on the reservation, many changes occurred in the lives and culture of the Shoshone. The reservation limited the area in which they could move and hunt food. Previously, the Indian man's role in the family had been to hunt game and foodstuffs for his family. However, with the creation of the reservation, the Indians were forced to get food from the government, for the reservation had an insufficient area for them to effectively hunt for food. The men suddenly found their role in the family meaningless. Their skills, which had gained them status in the family, were suddenly obsolete. The ways in which they had always achieved their self-esteem were no longer available to them.

Also, their culture had never permitted any expression of emotion with the exception of aggression towards outside enemies. When the culture no longer offered these alternative outlets for expression of aggression (buffalo hunting, intertribal warfare, etc.) and the traditional way of gaining self-esteem was no longer available, a high incidence of suicide occurred (Seiden, 1969).

The cultural changes prevented this group of Indians from dealing with their instinctual feelings, thus creating feelings of hopelessness and helplessness manifested through a higher suicide rate and other forms of self-destructive behavior, such as alcoholism, homicide (often victim precipitated), and "accidents" (Seiden, 1969).

From these studies, it can be concluded that culture factors can have a significant impact on suicidal behavior. While other variables that influence suicidal behavior are frequently considered, this very basic and important contributing factor can be easily overlooked.

## WEATHER

The influence of weather conditions on suicidal behavior has also been investigated. Mills (1934) studied the influence of fluctuations in barometric pressure and temperature on the incidence of suicide and homicide in North America. His study showed a high correlation between severe barometric pressure and temperature changes and suicide. The areas where "barometric pressure and temperature changes are most frequent and severe" are the areas where the suicide rate is highest (Mills, p. 676). He noted that the suicide rate is highest generally during a low pressure crisis. With falling barometric pressure and rising temperature, suicide rates rise. With rising barometric pressure and falling temperature, suicide rates decline.

Powers (1954a, 1956) reported that the incidence of suicide is lowest in the tropics and highest in the temperate zones and in the United States occurs most often in the North and least often in the South.

This research on weather suggests that weather conditions may influence suicidal behavior—another factor that might be overlooked.

From this review of the etiology of suicidal behavior, it is evident that many theories exist on what causes and/or influences suicidal behavior. However, as stated earlier in this book, no factor has been found to be solely responsible for causing suicidal behavior in adolescents. In the case of a seriously suicidal adolescent, while some specific situation may trigger the suicidal act, there has been a gradual buildup to that point.

Many factors that may contribute to subsequent suicidal behavior have been discussed in this chapter. The factors that appear to be most influential on suicidal behavior in adolescents are problems within the family, loss of a loved one (through death, divorce, or separation), depression, and social isolation. In the reviewed research, there is strong evidence that these four factors have the most significant impact on subsequent suicidal behavior by adolescents.

# CHAPTER 5

## PRODROMAL CLUES

OTTO (1964) stated, "Judging from the observations made on adults, there is reason to believe that a specific presuicidal syndrome does not exist" (p. 397). However, several other investigators presented numerous prodromal clues. Perlstein (1966) stated that of the serious suicide attempts, prodromal clues were present in over 70 percent of the cases. "The teenager who has reached the point of seriously considering suicide never fails to send out warning signals," stated Dr. Mary Giffin (O'Roark, 1982, p. 22). Parents, teachers, relatives, caregivers, and others in adolescents' lives must realize that these prodromal clues are a sign that help is needed. These prodromal clues are warning signals to potential suicidal behavior; they are a "cry for help." The following prodromal clues were presented by Perlstein (1966):

> The sleep disturbance may be insomnia or a tendency to excessive sleep. The eating disturbance often involves increased eating, increased tendency to take alcoholic beverages, increased smoking, or increased intake of sweets often reaching addictive proportions; but in other instances there is a loss of appetite and a decreased intake of food. Somatic symptoms include headache and pains of any type, asthenia, gastrointestinal complaints, tachycardia, menstrual complaints, and skin problems especially (p. 3018).

Hersh (1975) reported that a suicidal college student typically exhibits the following prodromal clues:

> a decrease in verbal communication combined with an increase in isolation (more isolation than usual for that individual); talk about giving away or actually giving away prized possessions; changes in the sleep

cycle (insomnia or sudden changes in the total amount of sleeping, especially during the day); active tensions with the family of origin (especially if there is evidence that psychological or physical abuse existed in that family) (p. 25).

Faigel (1966) stated that predicting the first suicide attempt was difficult. However, he listed the following prodromal clues: "attempts at suicide, accident proneness, recent death in the family, recent disruption of the family, repressed anger, deflated self-image, sex anxieties, and depression" (p. 189).

Jacobziner (1965a) cited the following prodromal clues: "change in personality or behavior, agitation, irritability, anxiety, depression, anorexia, insomnia, and frequent outbursts of temper" (p. 10). Frederick (1976), another investigator, stated—

Overt behavioral clues include actions such as purchasing a rope, guns, or pills. Covert behavioral clues are shown by loss of appetite, loss of weight, insomnia, disturbed sleep patterns, fatigue or loss of energy, isolated behavior, changes in mood, and increased irritability. Signs of deterioration are often revealed by a sudden change of behavior, which may not be flagrantly rebellious enough to include rule breaking and legal violations (p. 5).

While O'Roark (1982) mentioned many of the same prodromal clues as other investigators, she also urged teachers to watch for signs of suicide in creative writing and art. She stated that frequently students who are suicidal "become preoccupied with the notion of death in music, art, the poetry or journals they write" (p. 22).

Duncan (1977) pointed out that most suicide attempters have visited a physician with functional complaints in the months prior to the suicide attempt. Hyde and Forsyth's (1978) research also indicated that between 60 and 70 percent of the people who commit suicide have seen a medical doctor in the six months prior to their suicide, and Klagsbrun (1976) reported that 75 percent see a medical doctor within a month or two before they commit suicide. The problem is, however, that they conceal their suicidal intent from the physician and the physician either does not recognize the prodromal clues or does not attend to them (Klagsbrun, 1976).

The prodromal clues of suicide can be summarized in the following statements: (1) suicide threat or similar statement, (2) previous attempt, (3) depression, (4) sudden change in behavior or personality, (5) final arrangements, such as giving away treasured personal possessions, and (6) isolation.

If these prodromal clues go unnoticed, the cries for help generally continue to get louder and louder. Many adolescents have died from self-inflicted injuries because their cries for help were not heard or those who heard did not respond.

It is generally very difficult for individuals, particularly parents, to accept the fact that an adolescent may be suicidal, as most parents feel ultimately responsible for what happens to their child and suicide carries a very heavy burden of guilt for parents. So, even though parents and others may recognize these clues to suicidal behavior in an adolescent, the fact remains that it is normally very difficult for parents to believe that their child would even consider, much less commit, suicide.

# CHAPTER 6

# TREATMENT

A PHYSICIAN often becomes involved once a suicide attempt has been made. Powers (1954b) stated that the physician's attitude during that time is critical. Powers (1956) stated that if the physician judges the adolescent harshly at that point, communication with the adolescent will be more difficult, for the adolescent becomes isolated even further. On the other hand, if the physician is warm and accepting, the lines of communication between the physician and adolescent may be opened.

A number of investigators recommended hospitalization following a suicide gesture or attempt. Motto (1975) stated that conservatism is generally recommended as far as hospitalization is concerned. He suggested that "even if the attempt or gesture does not seem to be life-threatening, or if the episode appears to be 'just an attention-getting' device, hospitalization usually is indicated as a therapeutic measure" (p. 16). He stated that such action makes it clear to the adolescent that the cry for help has been heard and taken seriously.

Duncan (1977) also suggested hospitalization for an adolescent who has attempted suicide. Toolan (1968) too stated that a period of hospitalization is preferable, suggesting that hospitalization offers not only a protective setting for the adolescent but also allows the physician a chance to perform an evaluation before beginning treatment.

Gould (1965) suggested a number of measures, hospitalization being the first of them. He stated that hospitalization offers an escape "from pressures which precipitated the suicide attempt" (p. 241).

Gould (1965) suggested five other therapeutic measures: (1) Do not tell the patient that everything will be all right. He stated that such reassurance is empty and will only make the adolescent feel less self-esteem for having attempted suicide and feel anger and frustration because the communication was not understood. (2) Listen to the adolescent and take the individual seriously. The adolescent is trying desperately to communicate a message. If the cry is not heard, then another attempt may be made. (3) Do not do anything that might further diminish the adolescent's self-esteem. Any judgmental statements or criticism should be avoided. (4) Be available, particularly during the acute period when the adolescent may be suicidal. Even if there is some "manipulation" of the therapist, this is one instance where it should be tolerated until the relationship between the therapist and adolescent is stable and there is a trusting-working relationship. (5) Let the adolescent know that if the determination to commit suicide is there, the therapist is powerless to stop the act.

Motto (1975) suggested that the desired sequence of treatment is as follows:

> establishment of a dependency-gratifying relationship which the patient can accept without losing face, stimulation of emotional growth within this relationship, including the task of assisting the patient to become more self-sufficient without stirring fears of abandonment, and gradually diminishing the dependent aspects of the relationship at a pace consistent with the adolescent's maturation, accepting that some patients will require a degree of support almost indefinitely (p. 16).

His guidelines for facilitating these steps follow:

(1) In addition to the main therapist, other therapists should be used. This group can include any adult who is willing to listen and to try to understand the adolescent.

(2) Tailor the therapy to focus on the adolescent's unique problems and stresses. For example, if extreme dependency is a problem with the adolescent, attention should be focused on this problem and it should be examined from the adolescent's point of view.

(3) An emphasis should be placed on trying to stabilize the adolescent's emotional state by slowly trying to reestablish or

strengthen the relationships with parents and others.

(4) The adolescent's expectations of the therapeutic process must be explored. It must be made clear that no magical solutions exist and at the same time the therapist should try to maintain a role of authority.

(5) The adolescent should not be reassured that everything is all right. As stated earlier, such action may only serve to make the adolescent feel less self-esteem for attempting suicide and increase feelings of isolation and hopelessness. The adolescent may perceive such reassurance as evidence of failure by others to understand the communication.

(6) It must be clear to the adolescent that the therapist considers the situation serious and that by attempting suicide, he or she has not sacrificed self-respect and self-worth.

(7) Caution must be exercised in accepting the adolescent's assurances about future acts of self-destruction after a suicide attempt. The problem here is not one of honesty, but rather the individual may be so desperate to gain approval from adults and the need for immediate gratification may be so great that the adolescent cannot be expected to fairly predict behavior in the future.

(8) The therapist should be prepared for some very difficult times with the adolescent. Adolescents often have a lot of dependent-independent conflicts and also a lot of negative feeling about parental figures. These conflicts and feelings may arise during the therapy in such a way that it appears the adolescent is trying to make the therapist miserable rather than allowing the therapist to help. An adolescent's fear of dependence can interfere with the expression of gratitude or loving feelings and the adolescent may instead evidence demanding and criticizing behavior.

(9) The therapist should be as available as possible and approach both scheduling and the therapy process with as much flexibility as possible. While Motto (1975) pointed out that the adolescent may try to take advantage of this situation, until a firm relationship has developed, it is appropriate to allow a degree of manipulation. After the relationship between the adolescent and therapist has been established, then he suggested a more structured arrangement could be worked out.

(10) "The capacity to form meaningful relationships with others

is the most critical consideration in setting therapeutic goals, as social and emotional isolation are conducive to both limited emotional growth and to high risk for completed suicide" (Motto, p. 18). It is therefore critical that a network of meaningful relationships outside the therapeutic setting be developed by the adolescent.

(11) While tranquilizers and antidepressive drugs can be used for agitation and depression in nonpsychotic adolescents who are suicidal, they should not be used as a substitution for interpersonal ties and should not be prescribed in quantities that could be lethal if all are taken at once.

(12) Group therapy might be considered in addition to individual therapy. It would be preferable that the group therapist have an interest in suicide and some experience in the area. Motto pointed out that adolescents often feel persecuted by adults as well as by other adolescents and that peer support could be helpful in the therapeutic process.

(13) Family therapy is important for both progress and for stability over time. Minimal goals are an understanding of the treatment goals and risks and an investigation of the parent's role in the adolescent's behavior. He stated the family can also help by removing lethal weapons and agents from the home. When it is a primary source of stress, parental pressure may become the focal point of the family therapy.

(14) Dismissal from the hospital and follow-up treatment are critical steps. Much preparation is needed to make sure a supportive network is available at home and school. Follow-up should be continued for at least a year and after such time gradually diminished with the understanding that the therapist's door is always open. If the adolescent wishes to terminate therapy, Motto stated it is better to run the risk of having to later return to therapy than to stop an attempt by the adolescent to become more independent.

(15) Finally, if a suicide does occur, it is important for the therapist to have sufficient resources to provide the necessary help for the family. Such assistance can help the family deal with their guilt and anger and examine what, if anything, was done incorrectly. He suggested that this is preferably a staff function as opposed to a single staff member's effort.

Greuling and DeBlassie (1980) stated six indications of progress in therapy: "(1) increased outside interests, (2) increased peer relationships, both quantitatively and qualitatively, (3) improved family relationships, (4) improved self-concept, (5) improved academic function, (6) diminution of symptoms" (p. 600). They stressed that true progress in therapy and pseudoprogress should be differentiated. In the latter instance, the adolescent's symptoms disappear and the individual leaves therapy because of a fear of discovery of deeper problems. In such cases, anxiety is the main effect on the adolescent who leaves therapy. If the adolescent insists on leaving therapy, the therapist should politely disagree with the adolescent's decision and evaluation of the situation and make it clear that the adolescent is welcome to come back into therapy in the future. Greuling and DeBlassie (1980) stated that when this happens, a second attempt frequently occurs. If the attempt is not successful, the adolescent usually goes back into therapy.

Toolan (1968) reported that electroconvulsive therapy (ECT) is usually not as beneficial to depressed chldiren and adolescents as it is to adults. Toolan (1975) reported that ECT is seldom used in the treatment of depressed youngsters and that it should be used only when psychotherapy or antidepressant medication fails. He stated that antidepressant medication may help youngsters who show outward clinical signs of depression. He also stated that antidepressant medication may be of little value in a child or adolescent who is able to mask depression by acting out, although tricyclic antidepressants may be helpful to many who show outward clinical signs of depression or many who show somatic symptoms. He does report, however, that there is a lot of disagreement over the value of antidepressant drugs in treating children and adolescents.

Faigel (1966) stated that "the iminodibenzyl anti-depressants are very helpful in treating a depressed child" (p. 189). However, he further stated that drugs alone are not sufficient; psychotherapy is also required for the patient and family.

Gould (1965) stated that tranquilizers and antidepressants may be helpful to patients who are agitated and depressed. He suggested that the use of such drugs in treatment may prevent another suicide attempt before the benefits of psychotherapy and environmental changes are evident.

Duncan (1977) stated that drugs should be prescribed only in cases of psychotic disorders or severe anxiety or depression, assuming the patient is hospitalized. Otherwise, Duncan indicated, drug therapy is unwise because outpatients usually do not keep their appointments so their cases can be monitored by a physician. Duncan (1977) also stated that before an adolescent is released from the hospital, the parents should be instructed to remove all weapons from the home as well as other lethal agents.

Jacobziner (1960) stated that before an adolescent is released from the hospital, the community (including church) and family must be prepared for the adolescent's homecoming. They must be prepared to welcome the person back without any stigma. They need to understand that this is vital to the avoidance of future attempts.

Gould (1965) suggested that changes in the adolescent's environment would be advisable so that the adolescent does not have to return to the same stressful environment where the attempt was made. He stated that it is advisable to involve as many significant members of the family as possible in the treatment process. Further, "discouraging or encouraging certain activities and friendships, suggesting changes in school or curriculum and a variety of other interventions may be indicated to improve the milieu" (Gould, pp. 244-245). Gould (1965) also stated that if the situation at home is bad and cannot be changed, it would not be advisable to send the adolescent home but rather to a residential treatment center where there is no stress and where treatment is available.

Motto (1975) concluded his article on treating adolescents with the following:

> To the extent that the suicidal adolescent is met with consistent respect, concern, warm acceptance and a desire to understand his/her behavior and feelings, the risk of subsequent self-destructive actions will be reduced. It is primarily the development and nurturing of caring relationships that relieve the pain, rekindle hope, and finally generate the all-important feelings of relatedness to significant other persons that bind the adolescent willingly to life (p. 20).

Motto (1975) emphasized that how the treatment process is approached is generally more important than the treatment process selected.

While there are numerous treatment alternatives, it must be stressed that suicidal behavior warrants conservative treatment. In the case of the suicidal adolescent, conservative treatment is easily justified — the life of the adolescent is at stake. There is no room for error.

An added dimension to the treatment process for the professional is the matter of legal liability. Berman and Cohen-Sandler (1982) stated that while the matter of legal liability is generally a problem of the hospitals, the professional involved in the litigation is almost always a psychiatrist, as it is the psychiatrists who are at the top of the inpatient psychiatric hierarchy and in charge of the units.

In the thirty-seven suicidal malpractice cases reviewed, sixteen were won by the plaintiff. Berman and Cohen-Sandler (1982) reported that in each instance, the professional liability was determined basically on three factors: The foreseeability of a patient's suicide, reasonable care, and the dependability with which treatment orders are followed.

Berman and Cohen-Sandler stated that in regard to the first factor of professional liability, professionals are expected to make a prediction on the likelihood that a patient will commit suicide. However, the investigators stated that professionals "are not held legally responsible for errors in this subjective judgment unless standards of care are not met" (p. 117); that is, they will not be liable as long as they do not grossly misjudge the patient, considering the information available to them, or as long as they do not fail to provide reasonable care to a patient they judge to be highly suicidal.

With respect to the second factor, reasonable care is expected to be provided for the suicidal patient. As previously pointed out, if the patient is considered by the professional to be highly suicidal, it is expected that necessary precautions will be taken.

Thirdly, the treatment orders should be followed in a dependable fashion. The example Berman and Cohen-Sandler (1982) provided was an order that required a patient be escorted if leaving the unit. If the patient in such a case were to be allowed to leave without an escort, the order would obviously not have been followed and a case of negligence would be the result.

With these legal liability factors in mind, it is clear that if the professional makes every effort to assure that the patient receives optimal care, not only does the patient have the best chance to gain, but there is also less likelihood that the professional will lose in court.

schools. She pointed out that in both high schools and colleges, the response has been very good to courses on death and dying.

Greuling and DeBlassie (1980) reported that adolescents who are suicidal are not likely to talk with parents, clergymen, or others but may talk with a peer. They suggested that school counselors could increase their effectiveness by establishing themselves as a friend to whom the student can turn when facing problems. Greuling and De-Blassie (1980) felt that the school counselor could be of "life-saving service" in such a role.

Ross (1980) stated that a question on a survey on suicide conducted in a number of high schools revealed that students consistently responded that they would look to a peer for help if they were considering suicide rather than to a teacher, parent, school counselor, etc. As a result of her research, peer counseling programs were developed in the San Mateo County (California) school system.

Hart and Keidel (1979) stated that the school nurse "is in a unique position to help" (p. 82). There are numerous opportunities for the school nurse to help prevent suicide by adolescents. These opportunities include educating school personnel, students, and parents about suicide. The investigators suggested the following:

> This can be done by developing an inservice education program for teaching staff, working with an individual teacher who has a concern about a particular student, collaborating with the school guidance personnel, or speaking at junior high PTA meetings or to other groups. Nurses can become advocates for youth, for example, as volunteer leaders in organizations such as church, youth groups, 4-H clubs, or athletic associations. Or a nurse may want to become involved with organizations that have more formalized youth advocacy programs, such as runaway houses. A nurse could work toward having laws changed that require parental consent for medical care and/or information (pp. 82-83).

Hart and Keidel stated that the nurse needs to remember that it is important to get other individuals involved. The investigators stressed the importance of not keeping suggestions of suicidal behavior secret. They stated that the nurse could show concern by involving others. It is also important to involve others so that the nurse does not have to accept the burden of being solely responsible for the suicidal adolescent.

Jacobziner (1965a) stated that the community must provide more health agencies where individuals can get help and "motivate a concern for suicidal prevention" (p. 11).

Bennett (1957) outlined fifteen suggestions for suicide prevention: (1) Those who attempted suicide not only need emergency treatment but also further evaluation and follow-up so they will not attempt suicide again. Early diagnosis of depression is critical for those who have not attempted suicide. (2) Physicians must be more acquainted with the process of psychiatric referrals. They need to be influential in getting their patient the necessary treatment and protection. (3) In cases where no organic problem is observed in patients, physicians should seek signs of depression, as half of those who attempt suicide are psychoneurotically depressed. (4) Barbiturates should be very carefully prescribed and not prescribed in large quantities. (5) All suicide gestures and threats should be taken seriously and appropriate treatment arrangements should be provided.

(6) The public must be educated about suicide and the prodromal clues. Families should be careful not to take a patient out of the hospital too early merely because the patient wants to return home. The patient may want to go home to make another suicide attempt. (7) Lay organizations can help educate the public. Also, persons with suicidal impulses should be referred for treatment at available clinics. (8) Police officers should not only know how to give emergency treatment in the case of an attempted suicide but also how to get further help for the person and the family. (9) There needs to be more control and legal restraint over the prescribing of lethal and addictive drugs. (10) Hospital administrators should see that all persons treated in the emergency room for attempted suicide get a complete psychiatric evaluation and follow-up help.

(11) Suicide attempts should be reported the same as other diseases so that physicians and nurses can see that an individual gets proper follow-up treatment and care. (12) Psychiatrists and physicians should keep careful records to facilitate an understanding of the motives involved in suicidal behavior and to prevent attempts by others. (13) Since life insurance companies and accident insurance companies provide money for research for other diseases, these companies could furnish money for research on suicide. (14) Health in-

# CHAPTER 8

# INTERVENTION

INTERVENTION involves a personal relationship with a distressed person (Hart & Keidel, 1979, p. 83). This process may include talking with an adolescent who has been frequently involved in automobile accidents or other kinds of accidents about the adolescent's feelings and expressing concern for the individual (Hart and Keidel, 1979). At the most critical level, intervention may require direct physical action. Intervention should immediately follow any hint of a suicidal act or any suicidal clues (Hatton et al., 1977).

The four basic tasks of intervention for caregivers as outlined by Hatton et al. (1977) follow: (1) Establish a good rapport with the client. (2) Decide on the appropriate type of interview. She stressed that it is important that the client and family be seen together, as this offers the best chance of "promoting the health and stability of the family unit" (p. 72). (3) Intervention, as appropriate, should be based on lethality. (4) A verbal contract with the client should be made. In the contract, the client must promise not to commit any type of self-destructive behavior for a period of time, which is agreed upon by caregiver and client. Then, a plan for therapy should be made and the client should be directed to make whatever arrangements are necessary.

Berg (1972) stated that in a school setting, three different points of intervention are possible: (1) The teacher may intervene directly with the student. The teacher may confront the student in a very nice way and let the student know that the teacher realizes there is a problem. The first step toward solving the problem is creating an awareness.

(2) The second possible point of intervention is with the student's family. Berg stated that the teacher should not tell the family that the student may be suicidal but rather should simply point out that a major change has been noticed in the classroom.

(3) Berg also stated that another person should be made aware of the student's problem. He suggested that this person might be a school administrator, clergyman, or physician. He feels this is important, as talking with the student's family may not be successful and it is critical that the student be put in contact with someone to whom he or she can talk openly about feelings. Berg stated that the school administrator should establish a good relationship with those outside the school setting where help can be obtained. Sources in the community include hospitals, police, clinics, and physicians (Berg, 1972). He stated that the school administrator can be very influential in creating an environment that projects a positive influence toward dealing with emotional problems.

In cases where the suicidal student confides in a teacher, Schuyler (1973) urged teachers to listen and not be afraid to get involved. Referral sources vary depending upon the school, but Schuyler suggested that the school counselor is a good initial contact. He stated that the student's parents should be involved if possible (Schuyler, 1973).

Powers (1979) addressed the situation where a student makes a suicide threat or conveys some idea of self-destruction to a teacher. In this situation, Powers made the following suggestions: (1) The teacher should listen carefully to what the student says. The teacher should show concern and interest and should try to help. Excessive probing is not necessary, but it is important to try to find out if some particular event precipitated the feelings of self-destruction. Also, the teacher should try to determine if the student has communicated these feelings to anyone else. (2) A suicide threat should always be taken seriously—and not considered a manipulative effort—even though there may be some manipulation taking place.

(3) The teacher will have to decide the degree of urgency. Powers pointed out that the fact the adolescent has disclosed this information indicates that it is important for another person to know. He stated that although the adolescent may not wish that this informa-

tion be shared with parents, the teacher is responsible for doing so if it is determined that the parents should be informed. However, the principal should be informed and may be helpful in dealing with the student and parents. (4) The teacher and the school can be of help to the parents and adolescent by assisting them in obtaining the help of a professional.

(5) Powers pointed out that if help for the student is not available outside the school, the teacher can be of assistance by mobilizing help and a support system within the school; this would include the school counselor, other teachers, and other selected students. (6) It is desirable to have a liaison between the school and treatment facility if the adolescent is in treatment outside of school, although Powers stated that this is not always possible.

(7) If treatment outside of school is not possible, Powers suggested a consultative relationship between the teacher and a mental health professional could be very helpful. (8) A frequent concern of teachers is that of identifying students who might make a suicide attempt. In response to this problem, Powers suggested that teachers watch for a sudden change in behavior. For example, if a student who is normally very outgoing becomes very withdrawn, this could be a manifestation of depression. Powers pointed out that while a number of factors could be responsible for causing this change in behavior, it is advisable to explore what is going on with the student. Although the student may not be suicidal, the student may need help just as much as a suicidal student.

Pretzel (1972) stated that intervention may take place at any of six levels depending upon how far the person has progressed toward committing suicide: (1) The first level is the most critical point of intervention. At this level, physical action may be required to stop the person who is in the process of committing suicide. (2) At the second level, action such as making a gun or pills inaccessible to the person may be required. Here, no action has been taken by the potential suicide victim, but the person has decided to commit suicide. (3) At the third level of intervention, the person is suffering from much stress and needs assistance in getting some support resources organized. The caregiver can help the individual work out a plan to organize these resources or, if necessary, help the individual.

(4) The fourth level of intervention involves strengthening the in-

dividual's ego. This action can reduce the chance of suicidal behavior. For example, helping an adolescent who as a result of an injury is suddenly confined for life to a wheelchair realize that he or she is still a worthwhile person and can still lead a full life may very well prevent the person from committing some type of self-destructive behavior. (5) At the fifth level of intervention, the goal is to lessen stress as soon as it has been identified. In the case of a student, this may mean lightening the adolescent's school load to prevent the chance of suicidal behavior. (6) This last level of intervention, Pretzel stated, has been referred to as "primary prevention" by Doctor Norman Farberow. Intervention at this level involves maintaining the necessary social supports and services for the aged and those who are ill. Withdrawal of such support, Pretzel stated, would surely increase suicidal behavior.

An effective intervention technique with a potentially suicidal adolescent is simply talking with the adolescent about what is going on and how the individual is feeling. As noted earlier in this book, Sartore (1976) stated that discussing the topic of suicide does not implant a suicidal urge. In fact, O'Roark (1982) stated that talking about suicide with an adolescent who may be suicidal may serve to lessen the fear. As she stated, "Open up the subject. If you put a fear into words, it serves to defuse it. It transforms the fear into something tangible that can be dealt with. It's deadly not to talk about it" (p. 22).

Hart and Keidel (1979) said, "Speaking honestly about suicidal feelings and thoughts can be a catharsis for the isolated, unhappy young person" (p. 83). They further stated, "Detailed questions about the teenager's proposed plan of suicide can assist that person in ventilating feelings of depression" (p. 83).

While there are numerous types of intervention techniques, talking in a direct, calm, and nonjudgmental fashion with an adolescent about feelings can be a very effective technique that should not be overlooked.

It is important to remember that intervention should follow any hint of a suicidal act or any suicidal clue. Suicidal behavior is difficult to predict. Time may run out; therefore, it is important to act and to act immediately.

A second critical fact of intervention is remembering every

...mpt must be taken seriously. Even though the
...ay be a manipulative effort or partially a manip-
...is important to remember this cannot be the main
con...

The ...d fact of intervention to remember is that while there are
many intervention techniques, talking with an adolescent who may
be suicidal about how the individual is feeling and about suicide can
be very effective. Such intervention serves to lessen the fear and can
help ventilate feelings of depression. This, of course, should be done
in a very calm, direct, and nonjudgmental fashion.

While the reviewed research indicates that intervention may take
place at many levels, the preferable level of intervention is that of
maintaining and providing for adolescents the support, love, care,
and understanding they need to successfully handle stresses, conflicts, tensions, pressures, difficulties, and adjustments, which are
part of the developmental stage of adolescence.

# CHAPTER 9

## POSTVENTION

THE suicidal death of a family member, particularly of a child, has a tremendous emotional impact on a family. Farberow (1968) reported that the intensity of the emotional reactions is generally directly related to the distance of the relationship between the survivor and victim. In the case of an adolescent, Herzog and Resnik (1968) observed that the "immediate parental response to this sudden loss appears to be overwhelming hostility and denial, followed by guilt and depression" (p. 384). Farberow (1968) noted that the range of emotions experienced by relatives, friends, family members, and the therapist may include the following:

> (1) strong feelings of loss, accompanied by sorrow and mourning; (2) strong feelings of anger for (a) being made to feel responsible, or (b) being rejected in that what was offered was refused; (3) guilt, shame, or embarrassment with feelings of responsibility for the death; (4) feelings of failure or inadequacy that what was needed could not be supplied; (5) feelings of relief that the nagging, insistent demands have ceased; (6) feelings of having been deserted, especially true for children; (7) ambivalence, with a mixture of all the above; (8) reactions of doubt and self-questioning whether enough was attempted; (9) denial that a suicide has occurred, with a possible conspiracy of silence among all concerned; and (10) arousal of one's own impulses toward suicide (p. 394).

To help the survivors of a suicide deal with these emotions, a mental health intervention is recommended. Edwin Shneidman has referred to this process as "postvention" (Hatton et al., 1977, p. 120). Hatton et al. (1977) reported, "According to Shneidman, postvention is comprised of those activities following the death of a significant other by suicide that serve to assist survivors in coping with their emotional and psychologic response to the loss" (p. 120). The investigators further stated that Shneidman believes "the focus of postvention is not limited to the initial stages of shock and disbelief, but rather is directed toward bereavement as it is experienced in daily living by the survivor" (p. 120).

Cantor (1975) also reported, "The aim of postvention is to help the survivors to work through their feelings of grief which invariably accompany a death" (p. 8).

Herzog and Resnik (1968) outlined the three Rs of preventative mental health for the survivors of a suicidal death: psychologic resuscitation, psychologic rehabilitation, and psychologic renewal. The three Rs represent the three stages of Resnik's psychologic resynthesis. The following paragraphs outline the goal and purpose of each of these three stages.

The first stage of the postvention process is psychologic resuscitation. Herzog and Resnik (1968) stated that within twenty-four hours of the suicide, an intervenor should visit with the survivors. They recommend that this visit be made by a mental health professional rather than someone who might be identified as a member of the medical examiner's office. Hatton et al. (1977) outlined the goals of this first visit with the survivors: "(1) To establish rapport with the survivors (2) To help the survivors withstand the initial shock of their immense loss (3) To help the survivors become aware of their basic emotions at this time — their feelings of confusion, guilt, and blame, and often their strong feelings of hostility and perhaps severe depression" (p. 126). The investigators also stated that the mental health professional should not force the family to accept the death as a suicide if they are not ready to do so.

The second stage of the postvention process is psychologic rehabilitation. Hatton et al. (1977) stated that this stage normally begins after the funeral when the mental health professional visits the survivors again. They outlined the goals of this second stage as follows:

(1) To make a contract with the family establishing regular meeting times with them, either with individual members alone or in group as a unit, and either in the home or at the office (sometimes a combination of these), covering the first six months of the first year following the suicide (2) To support the reintegration of the family (3) To help the fam-

ily deal with the period of mourning and the grief process, and to help
them understand the dynamics of grieving (4) To deal with whatever
emotions or social problems or crises may arise during this period (p.
126).

After a six-month period has elapsed, the third stage of psychologic renewal begins. At this time, contacts with the mental health
professional are limited to the times when the family contacts the
mental health professional (Herzog and Resnik, 1968). This third
stage ends on the first anniversary of the suicide (Herzog and Resnik, 1968). On the anniversary date, the mental health professional
contacts the family again, and Herzog and Resnik (1968) stated that
this visit normally reopens the grieving process for a short period of
time. The purpose of this visit by the mental health professional is to
let the family know that the therapist realizes that the date is significant to the family (Herzog and Resnik, 1968).

Powers (1979) suggested that in the case of a student suicide, the
school administration may find it helpful to bring in a mental health
professional to talk with faculty and students and to involve the
school counselor. He stressed that if group discussions on suicide
were conducted in order to help all individuals deal with their emotions, the privacy and dignity of the surviving family members must
be protected.

Powers (1979) further stated that such a group discussion would
most likely want to focus on three major areas: (1) the grieving process and the emotions experienced by those involved, (2) the many
complex factors that make up a person's personality and the many
precipitating circumstances that may lead to a suicidal death, and
(3) the prodromal clues, which may warn a teacher that a student is
extremely vulnerable and how the teacher may help.

In a school setting when a student confides in a teacher about a
death in the student's family, Schuyler (1973) urged teachers to get
the student into a counseling situation. Such action, Schuyler (1973)
stated, may prevent many negative aftereffects of a suicidal death.
Aftereffects may take the form of depression, a suicide attempt on
the anniversary date of the family member's death, etc. (Schuyler,
1973).

Berg (1972) stated that in the case where a student has attempted suicide, the teacher can help reduce feelings of isolation by communicating with the student. In the case of a student suicide, Berg (1972) recommended that a discussion of the situation in the classroom would give other students a chance to share how the suicide has affected them and hopefully reduce the chance of another suicide or an epidemic of suicides by students. He also urged school administrators to encourage discussions of a suicidal death among teachers with the hope of putting together a plan to help lessen the isolation of a student who attempted suicide or to help lessen the isolation of the family of a student who committed suicide.

Berg (1972) urged teachers, after a suicide has taken place, to discuss the situation in the classroom. This would allow students to share their feelings and ideas. He pointed out that the students in school will be talking about suicide "but otherwise in ignorance and fear" (p. 231).

Herzog and Resnik (1968) stated that suicide by survivors and anniversary suicides are a fact of suicidology. Shneidman (1981) reported that statistics indicate "survivors are apt to have a higher morbidity and mortality rate in the year following the death of their loved one than comparable persons who are not survivors of such a death" (p. 220). The difficulty that survivors encounter in dealing with a suicide is reflected in the statistics to which Shneidman has made reference. These statistics support the need for mental health intervention in the case of a suicidal death.

The importance of postvention, particularly in the case of an adolescent suicide, cannot be overemphasized. "The parents of children who commit suicide are plagued by deep, unresolved guilt and prolonged periods of depression. The fathers especially appear to need help in adjusting to the suicidal death of their child" (Herzog and Resnik, 1968, p. 385).

Survivors need the opportunity to work through the emotional turmoil that results from a suicidal death. "Thus postvention affords an opportunity for the expression of guarded emotions, especially of those negative affective states such as anger, guilt, and shame. This process brings a measure of stability to the grieving person's life and at the very least provides a genuine interpersonal relationship in which honest thoughts and feelings can be expressed" (Hatton et al.

1977, p. 120).

Postvention not only helps the survivors of a suicide cope with the emotions that accompany the tragedy but also aids in reducing the chances of an anniversary suicide or a suicide by a survivor.

# CHAPTER 10

# SUMMARY

WHILE a review of the history of suicide revealed a broad range of social attitudes over the years and within societies, a range of attitudes toward suicide still exists in American society today. Recognizing, however, that it is an accepted fact of suicidology that many suicides in our country are not reported because of religious, social, and legal taboos, one can conclude that the prevailing attitude toward suicidal behavior in our society today is one of disapproval.

Since the reviewed research indicated that the number of committed suicides that go unreported for children and adolescents is even higher than for adults, one can also conclude that suicidal behavior in young people is considered even more taboo. However, it should be remembered that underreporting also occurs more frequently in children and adolescents because of parents' inability to deal with their own feelings and responsibility for what has happened to their children.

While adolescence is often considered as the time in life when young people "have all the fun" before becoming saddled with all the responsibilities of adulthood, in reality, the research has indicated that adolescence is not that at all. Adolescence has been described in the literature as "a critical period associated with many emotional and social conflicts, tensions, pressures, stresses, and home and school difficulties" (Jacobziner, 1960, p. 523). It is during this time that investigators have stated that adolescents are faced with the task of establishing a sense of personal identity.

While the literature presented a number of ways in which adolescents may choose to cope with the problems they experience, suicide was given as one of the alternatives. In an effort to explain why some adolescents choose suicide over other alternatives, a closer examination of who attempts suicide and who commits suicide was made.

The literature revealed that for years investigators grouped all suicidal behavior together regardless of the nature of the act or the intent of the person committing the act. Recently, however, investigators have begun to believe there are both specific differences and commonalities between these two groups. Prior to the time investigators began separating these two populations, attempted suicide was viewed simply as a suicide attempt that failed.

The research indicated that only a small portion of those who attempt suicide go on to commit suicide. It was also reported that there are many more attempted suicides than committed suicides. A reason given for the disproportionately higher number of attempted suicides than committed suicides was that attempted suicide is often believed to be an effort to gain attention or to manipulate others rather than an actual desire to die. Investigators have suggested that many who attempt suicide have no intention of dying; for them the suicide attempt is a cry for help and a plea to be noticed. In such instances, frequently the method chosen for the attempt allows for the greatest chance of rescue. Even then, these attempts are sometimes accidentally successful. If a cry for help is not answered, investigators reported that it is often repeated in a more serious way. Many adolescents are believed to have died because their cries for help were not answered or those who heard did not respond.

The reviewed literature indicated that those who attempt suicide are generally younger, use more passive methods, use less lethal methods, and have no desire to die. The motivation underlying the action in such cases is more frequently of a manipulative or attention-seeking nature. On the other hand, the literature indicated that those who commit suicide are generally older, use more lethal methods, are more isolated, feel more hopeless, are less likely to give out warning signals for help, have a history of more frequent psychiatric hospitalization, are more emotionally disturbed, have made fewer prior attempts, and have more of a disposition toward self-destruction and thus require less overt stress from their peers to trigger the suicide act.

Statistics indicated that while females are responsible for between 75 and 90 percent of all attempted suicides by adolescents, males are responsible for 80 percent of all committed suicides by adolescents. One of the reasons for these statistics was reported to be because males have traditionally used more lethal methods. Other reasons are that it is socially more acceptable for females to ask for help when they have problems and females tend to act more impulsively, thus their attempts are not as well planned and therefore are not as successful. Also, although females attempt suicide much more often than males, they frequently have less desire to die.

Many possible causes for suicidal behavior were examined in this book. However, no single cause was found to be solely responsible for suicidal behavior in adolescents. The factors identified as most influential on subsequent suicidal behavior were (1) problems within the family, (2) loss of a loved one (through death, divorce, or separation), (3) depression, and (4) social isolation.

A major concern of caregivers, parents, and others in contact with adolescents was reportedly identifying potentially suicidal adolescents. Investigators presented numerous prodromal clues intended to help these individuals with this concern. These prodromal clues were summarized as follows: (1) a suicide threat or similar statement, (2) a previous attempt, (3) depression, (4) sudden change in behavior or personality, (5) final arrangements, such as giving away treasured personal possessions, and (6) isolation. The point was also made that even though parents may recognize these clues in an adolescent, the fact remains that it is frequently very difficult for them to believe their child would even consider, much less commit, suicide. This problem was attributed to the fact that parents generally feel ultimately responsible for what happens to their children, and suicide carries with it a heavy burden of guilt for parents.

Investigators generally agreed that conservative treatment is recommended for those who attempt suicide. Specifically, hospitalization for someone who has made a suicide attempt was recommended. In such instances, hospitalization was reported to serve the following purposes: (1) It makes it clear to the adolescent that the cry for help has been heard and taken seriously; (2) it offers a protective setting; (3) it allows the physician to make an evaluation before beginning treatment; and (4) it offers an escape from the situation that precipitated the attempt.

Parents, caregivers, and others in contact with adolescents who have made a suicide attempt were reminded that a nonjudgmental, respectful, concerned, and accepting attitude toward these adolescents is critical. It was also suggested that these individuals not reassure the adolescents that everything will be all right because such reassurance is devoid of meaning. As a result, adolescents tend to feel less self-esteem for having attempted suicide and anger and frustration because their communication was not understood. Caregivers were urged to remember that it is important to be available to the adolescent, particularly during the period when the adolescent is suicidal. Even if there is some manipulation taking place, this is one instance where it should be tolerated until a stable, trusting-working relationship has developed between the adolescent and the caregiver.

Indications of progress in therapy with adolescents were reported to include the following: (1) more outside interests, (2) an increase in the number and quality of peer relationships, (3) better relationships with family members, (4) a better self-concept, (5) a better academic function, and (6) a decrease of symptoms.

A major issue concerning the prevention of suicidal behavior was that of educating parents, caregivers, and others in contact with adolescents on the problems and needs of adolescents, how to recognize the prodromal clues, and what to do if they suspect an adolescent may be suicidal. Before parents, caregivers, and others in contact with adolescents can recognize and deal with suicidal behavior, the point was made that they must be knowledgeable about suicide.

Other factors to help with the prevention of suicidal behavior in adolescents included teaching children coping skills through parental role modeling and problem-solving techniques. The showing of care and concern for unhappy adolescents was also emphasized. A final issue in the prevention of suicidal behavior was that of confidentiality. In the case of potential suicidal behavior, everyone was reminded that the prime concern is the preservation of life, even if it requires a breach of confidence.

The many different levels of intervention were discussed at

length. The important point to be remembered is that intervention should immediately follow any hint of a suicidal act or any suicidal clues. Every suicide threat or attempt must be taken seriously even though there may be some manipulation taking place. While there are many intervention techniques, the effectiveness of talking with an adolescent about suicide and how he or she is feeling should be remembered. This, of course, must be done in a very calm, direct, and nonjudgmental manner.

The preferable level of intervention, of course, is that of maintaining and providing adolescents the support, love, care, and understanding they need to successfully handle stresses, conflicts, tensions, pressures, difficulties, and adjustments, which are part of the developmental stage of adolescence.

In the case of a suicidal death, a mental health intervention was recommended. This process is postvention. The purpose of postvention, as described in Chapter 9, is to help the survivors cope with their emotional and psychologic response to the loss that they have experienced. Not only does this process allow the survivors an opportunity to work through their emotional turmoil, but it also aids in reducing the chances of an anniversary suicide or suicide by a survivor. Such deaths are a fact of suicidology, and postvention is a way of helping to minimize the chances of such a death.

Adolescent suicide has become a national tragedy. The number of suicides continues to grow. With the information in this book, caregivers, parents, and others in contact with adolescents can take the first step toward addressing this tragedy, that is, they can obtain a better understanding of suicidal behavior in adolescents and can learn how to recognize and respond to this type of behavior.

# CHAPTER 11

# RECOMMENDATIONS FOR THOSE IN CONTACT WITH ADOLESCENTS

THE following specific recommendations are made for those in contact with adolescents:

1. Learn the prodromal clues of suicide.

2. If an adolescent exhibits any of these prodromal clues, allow yourself to believe that the adolescent may be suicidal. If an adolescent confides in you feelings of being "better off dead" (or makes some similar type of statement), allow yourself to believe that the adolescent may be suicidal.

3. In either instance, talk freely, calmly, and directly with the adolescent about these feelings. Ask questions about how long the adolescent has felt this way, whether the adolescent has considered how the act would be carried out, whether the adolescent has a suicide plan, whether the adolescent has acquired the means, etc. No judgmental remarks should be made and the adolescent should not be reassured that "everything is OK." Do not get involved in any argument about life vs. death. Listen carefully to what the adolescent says and try to understand what the adolescent is feeling. Remember that as a *general* rule, the more specific the suicidal plan, the higher the risk. Also remember that suicidal individuals are generally very honest about their feelings and intentions.

---

This information is also found in "Suicide and How to Prevent It" (1977) and "What You Can Do" (1977).

4. Get professional help for the adolescent regardless of any denial of intent to commit suicide. If the adolescent is in any immediate danger, do not leave the adolescent alone.

5. *DO SOMETHING.*

# REFERENCES

Alvarez, A.: *The Savage God.* New York, Bantam, 1972.

Babow, Irving, and Kridle, Robin: Problems and encounters of a suicidal adolescent girl. *Adolescence, 7(28)*:459-478, 1972.

Bakwin, Harry: Suicide in children and adolescents. *Journal of Pediatrics, 50(6)*:749-769, 1957.

Bakwin, Ruth Morris: Suicide in children and adolescents. *Journal of the American Medical Women's Association, 28(12)*:643-650, 1973.

Balser, Benjamin H., and Masterson, James F., Jr.: Suicide in adolescents. *American Journal of Psychiatry, 116(5)*:400-404, 1959.

Barter, James T., Swaback, Dwight O., and Todd, Dorothy: Adolescent suicide attempts. *Archives of General Psychiatry, 19*:523-527, 1968.

Beeley, A.L.: Juvenile suicide. *Social Service Review, 3(1)*:35-49, 1929.

Bennett, A.E.: Suggestions for suicide prevention. In Shneidman, Edwin S., and Farberow, Norman L. (Eds.): *Clues to Suicide.* New York, McGraw, 1957.

Berg, Donald E.: A plan for preventing student suicide. *Self Destructive Behavior—A National Crisis.* Minneapolis, Burgess, 1972.

Bergstrand, C.G., and Otto, Ulf: Suicidal attempts in adolescence and childhood. *Acta Paediatrica, 51(1)*:17-26, 1962.

Berman, Alan L., and Cohen-Sandler, Roni: Suicide and the standard of care: Optimal vs. acceptable. *Suicide and Life-Threatening Behavior, 12(2)*:114-122, 1982.

Bigras, Julian, Gauthier, Yvon, Bouchard, Colette, and Tasse, Yolande: Suicidal attempts in adolescent girls: A preliminary study. *Canadian Psychiatric Association Journal (Suppl.)*:275-282, 1966.

Braaten, Leif J., and Darling, C. Douglas: Suicidal tendencies among college students. *Psychiatric Quarterly, 36(4)*:665-692, 1962.

Bruyn, Henry B., and Seiden, Richard H.: Student suicide: Fact or fancy? *Journal of the American College Health Association, 14(2)*:69-77, 1965.

Cantor, Pamela: The adolescent attempter: Sex, sibling position, and family constellation. *Life-Threatening Behavior, 2(4)*:252-261, 1972.

75

Cantor, Pamela: The effects of youthful suicide on the family. *Psychiatric Opinion, 12(6)*:6-11, 1975.

Corder, Billie F., Shorr, Walter, and Corder, Robert F.: A study of social and psychological characteristics of adolescent suicide attempters in an urban, disadvantaged area. *Adolescence, 9(33)*:1-6, 1974.

Cull, John G., and Gill, Wayne S.: *Suicide Probability Scale (SPS)* (psychological test). Los Angeles, Western Psychological Services, 1982.

Dizmang, Larry H., Watson, Jane, May, Philip A., and Bopp, John: Adolescent suicide at an Indian reservation. *American Journal of Orthopsychiatry, 44(1)*:43-49, 1974.

Dorpat, Theodore L., Jackson, Joan K., and Ripley, Herbert S.: Broken homes and attempted and committed suicide. *Archives of General Psychiatry, 12(2)*:213-216, 1965.

Dublin, Louis I.: *Suicide: A Sociological and Statistical Study*. New York, Ronald, 1963.

Duncan, Jane Watson: The immediate management of suicide attempts in children and adolescents: Psychologic aspects. *Journal of Family Practice, 4(1)*:77-80, 1977.

Faigel, Harris C.: Suicide among young persons. A review of its incidence and causes, and methods for its prevention. *Clinical Pediatrics, 5*:187-190, 1966.

Farberow, Norman L.: Suicide: Psychological aspects. *The International Encyclopedia of the Social Sciences, 15*:390-396, 1968.

Ford, Richard: Death by hanging of adolescent and young adult males. *Journal of Forensic Sciences, 2(2)*:171-176, 1957.

Frederick, Calvin J.: *Trends in Mental Health: Self-Destructive Behavior Among Younger Age Groups*. Rockville, MD, Department of Health, Education, and Welfare, Publication No. (ADM) 76-365, 1976.

French guide to suicide is chided and derided. *The Kansas City Star*, September 12, 1982, p. J-5.

Gentry, Bobbie: *Ode to Billy Joe* (phonograph record). Capital Records, 1967.

Glaser, Kurt: Attempted suicide in children and adolescents: Psychodynamic observations. *American Journal of Psychotherapy, 19(2)*:220-227, 1965.

Gorceix, A.: Le suicide, l'adolescence et le poison (suicide, adolescence and poison). *Semaine des Hopitaux de Paris, 39(50)*:2371-2374, 1963.

Gould, Robert E.: Suicide problems in children and adolescents. *American Journal of Psychotherapy, 19(2)*:228-246, 1965.

Greer, Steven: The relationship between parental loss and attempted suicide: A control study. *British Journal of Psychiatry, 110(468)*:698-705, 1964.

Greuling, Jacquelin W., and DeBlassie, Richard R.: Adolescent suicide. *Adolescence, 15(59)*:589-601, 1980.

Hart, Nancy A., and Keidel, Gladys C.: The suicidal adolescent. *American Journal of Nursing, 79(1)*:80-84, 1979.

Hatton, Corrine Loing, Valente, Sharon McBride, and Rink, Alice: *Suicide: Assessment and Intervention*. New York, Appleton-Century-Crofts, 1977.

Hazel, J.S., Schumaker, J.B., Sherman, J.A., and Sheldon-Wildgen, J.: *Asset: A*

*Social Skills Program for Adolescents.* Champaign, IL, Res Press, 1981.

Hendin, Herbert: Growing up dead: Student suicide. *American Journal of Psychotherapy, 29*:327-338, 1975(a).

Hendin, Herbert: Student suicide: Death as a life style. *The Journal of Nervous and Mental Disease, 160*:204-219, 1975(b).

Hendin, Herbert: *Suicide in America.* New York, Norton, 1982.

Hersh, Stephen P.: Suicide: Youth's high vulnerability to it — signs to look for — how you can help. *Mental Health, 59(3)*:23-25, 1975.

Herzog, Alfred, and Resnik, H.L.P.: A clinical study of parental response to adolescent death by suicide with recommendations for approaching the survivors. In Farberow, Norman L. (Ed.): *Proceedings of the Fourth International Conference for Suicide Prevention*, Los Angeles, CA, Suicide Prevention Center, Inc., Delmar Pub. Co., Inc., 1968. pp. 381-390.

Holzinger, Paul C.: Adolescent suicide: An epidemiological study of recent trends. *American Journal of Psychiatry, 135(6)*:754-756, 1978.

Hyde, Margaret O., and Forsyth, Elizabeth Held: *Suicide: The Hidden Epidemic.* New York, Watts, 1978.

Iga, Mamoru: Suicide of Japanese youth. *Suicide and Life-Threatening Behavior, 11(1)*:17-30, 1981.

Jacobs, Jerry, and Teicher, Joseph D.: Broken homes and social isolation in attempted suicide of adolescents. *International Journal of Social Psychiatry, 13(2)*:139-149, 1967.

Jacobziner, Harold: Attempted suicide in children. *Journal of Pediatrics, 56(4)*:519-525, 1960.

Jacobziner, Harold: Attempted suicides in adolescence. *Journal of the American Medical Association, 191(1)*:7-11, 1965(a).

Jacobziner, Harold: Attempted suicides in adolescents by poisonings: Statistical report. *American Journal of Psychotherapy, 19(2)*:247-252, 1965(b).

Kallmann, Franz J., and Anastasio, Mary M.: Twin studies on the psychopathology of suicide. *Journal of Heredity, 37*:171-180, 1946.

Kallmann, Franz J., De Porte, Joseph, De Porte, Elizabeth, and Feingold, Lissy: Suicide in twins and only children. *American Journal of Human Genetics, 1*:113-126, 1949.

Klagsbrun, Francine: *Too Young To Die.* Boston, HM, 1976.

LaVoie, Joseph C.: Ego identity formation in middle adolescence. *Journal of Youth and Adolescence, 5(4)*:371-385, 1976.

Lester, David: Fear of death of suicidal persons. *Psychological Reports (Part 2), 20(3)*:1077-1078, 1967.

Litman, Robert E., Curphey, Theodore, Shneidman, Edwin S., Farberow, Norman L., and Tabachnick, Norman: Investigations of equivocal suicides. *Journal of the American Medical Association, 184*:924-929, 1963.

Lyman, J.L.: Student suicide at Oxford University. *Student Medicine, 10(2)*:218-234, 1961.

McAnarney, Elizabeth R.: Adolescent and young adult suicide in the United States: A reflection of societal unrest. *Adolescence, 14(56)*:765-774, 1979.

Miller, John P.: Suicide and adolescence. *Adolescence, 10(37)*:11-24, 1975.

Mills, C.A.: Suicides and homicides in their relation to weather changes. *American Journal of Psychiatry, 91*:669-677, 1934.

Mishara, Brian L.: The extent of adolescent suicidality. *Psychiatric Opinion, 12(6)*:32-37, 1975.

Moss, Leonard M., and Hamilton, Donald C.: The psychotherapy of the suicidal patient. *American Journal of Psychiatry, 112*:814-820, 1956.

Motto, Jerome: Suicide and suggestibility — the role of the press. *American Journal of Psychiatry, 124(2)*:252-256, 1967.

Motto, Jerome A.: Treatment and management of suicidal adolescents. *Psychiatric Opinion, 12(6)*:14-20, 1975.

Neuringer, Charles: Problems in predicting adolescent suicidal behavior. *Psychiatric Opinion, 12(6)*:27-31, 1975.

O'Roark, Mary Ann: The alarming rise in teenage suicide. *McCalls*, January 1982, pp. 14, 16, 22, 120.

Otto, Ulf: Changes in the behavior of children and adolescents preceding suicidal attempts. *Acta Psychiatrica Scandinavica, 40(4)*:386-400, 1964.

Otto, Ulf: Suicidal attempts made by children and adolescents because of school problems. *Acta Paediatrica Scandinavica, 54(4)*:348-356, 1965.

Paffenbarger, Ralph S., and Asnes, Daniel P.: Chronic disease in former college students. III. Precursors of suicide in early and middle life. *American Journal of Public Health, 56*:1026-1036, 1966.

Parnell, R.W.: Mortality and prolonged illness among Oxford undergraduates. *Journal-Lancet, 260(6657)*:731-733, March 31, 1951.

Parrish, Henry M.: Epidemiology of suicide among college students. *Yale Journal of Biology and Medicine, 29*:585-595, 1957.

Peck, Michael L.: Suicide motivations in adolescents. *Adolescence, 3(9)*:109-118, 1968.

Peck, Michael L., and Schrut, Albert: Suicidal behavior among college students. *HSMHA Health Reports, 86(2)*:149-156, February 1971.

Peck, Michael L.: Teenage suicide — A tragic impulse. *MD*, February 1981, pp. 49-52.

Peck, Michael L.: When a teenager gets really depressed. *Changing Times*, June 1982, pp. 27-28.

Perlstein, Abraham P.: Suicide in adolescence. *New York State Journal of Medicine, 66(23)*:3017-3020, 1966.

Powers, Douglas: Youthful suicide attempts. *Northwest Medicine, 53(10)*:1001-1002, 1954(a).

Powers, Douglas: Youthful suicide attempts. *Northwest Medicine, 53(10)*:1231-1232, 1954(b).

Powers, Douglas: Suicide threats and attempts in the young. *American Practitioner, 7(7)*:1140-1143, 1956.

Powers, Douglas: The teacher and the adolescent suicide threat. *The Journal of School Health, 49(10)*:561-563, 1979.

Pretzel, Paul W.: *Understanding and Counseling the Suicidal Person*. Nashville, Abingdon, 1972.

Raphael, Theophile, Power, Sadye H., and Berridge, W. Lloyd: The question of suicide as a problem in college mental hygiene. *American Journal of Orthopsychiatry, 7(1)*:1-14, 1937.

Rice, F. Philip: *The Adolescent*, 3rd ed. Boston, Allyn, 1981.

Rook, Alan: Student suicides. *British Medical Journal, 5122*:599-603, 1959.

Rosenkrantz, Arthur L.: A note on adolescent suicide: Incidence, dynamics and some suggestions for treatment. *Adolescence, 13(50)*:209-214, 1978.

Ross, Charlotte P.: Mobilizing schools for suicide prevention. *Suicide and Life-Threatening Behavior, 10(4)*:239-243, 1980.

Sabbath, Joseph C.: The suicidal adolescent: The expendable child. *Journal of the American Academy of Child Psychiatry, 8(2)*:272-285, 1969.

Sartore, Richard L.: Students and suicide: An interpersonal tragedy. *Theory into Practice, 15(5)*:337-339, 1976.

Schechter, Marshall D.: The recognition and treatment of suicide in children. In Shneidman, Edwin S., and Farberow, Norman L. (Eds.): *Clues to Suicide*. New York, McGraw, 1957.

Schneer, Henry I., Kay, Paul, and Brozovsky, Morris: Events and conscious ideation leading to suicidal behavior in adolescence. *Psychiatric Quarterly, 35(3)*:507-515, 1961.

Schonfeld, William A.: Socioeconomic influence as a factor. *New York State Journal of Medicine, 67(14)*:1981-1990, 1967.

Schrut, Albert: Suicidal adolescents and children. *The Journal of the American Medical Association, 188(13)*:1103-1107, 1964.

Schuyler, Dean: When was the last time you took a suicidal child to lunch? *Journal of School Health, 43(8)*:504-506, 1973.

Seiden, Richard H.: Campus tragedy: A study of student suicide. *Journal of Abnormal Psychology, 71(6)*:389-399, 1966.

Seiden, Richard H.: *Suicide Among Youth*. Public Health Service Publication, No. 1971, December 1969.

Shankel, L. Willard and Carr, Arthur C.: Transvestism and hanging episodes in a male adolescent. *Psychiatric Quarterly, 30(1)*:478-493, 1956.

Shapiro, Louis B.: Suicide: Psychology and family tendency. *Journal of Nervous and Mental Disease, 81*:547-553, 1935.

Shneidman, Edwin S.: Suicide. *Suicide and Life-Threatening Behavior, 11(4)*:198-220, 1981.

Shneidman, Edwin S., and Farberow, Norman L.: Clues to suicide. In Shneidman, Edwin S., and Farberow, Norman L. (Eds.): *Clues to Suicide*. New York, McGraw, 1957.

Stearns, A. Warren: Cases of probable suicide in young persons without obvious motivation. *Journal of the Maine Medical Association, 44(1)*:16-23, 1953.

Stengel, Erwin: *Suicide and Attempted Suicide*. Bristol, England, MacGibbon & Kee Ltd., 1965.

Suicide and How to Prevent It (brochure). West Point, PA, Merck, Sharp & Dohme, 1977.

Swanson, David W.: Suicide in identical twins. *American Journal of Psychiatry*,

*116(1)*:934-935, 1960.

Teicher, Joseph D., and Jacobs, Jerry: Adolescents who attempt suicide: Preliminary findings. *American Journal of Psychiatry, 122(11)*:1248-1257, 1966.

Tishler, Carl L., McKenry, Patrick C., and Morgan, Karen Christman: Adolescent suicide attempts: Some significant factors. *Suicide and Life-Threatening Behavior, 11(2)*:86-92, 1981.

Toolan, James M.: Suicide and suicidal attempts in children and adolescents. *American Journal of Psychiatry, 118(8)*:719-724, 1962.

Toolan, James M.: Suicide in childhood and adolescence. In Resnik, H.L.P. (Ed.): *Suicidal Behaviors*. London, J. & A. Churchill Ltd., 1968.

Toolan, James M.: Suicide in children and adolescents. *American Journal of Psychotherapy, 29(3)*:339-344, 1975.

Tooley, Kay M.: The remembrance of things past: On the collection and recollection of ingredients useful in the treatment of disorders resulting from unhappiness, rootlessness, and the fear of things to come. *American Journal of Orthopsychiatry, 48(1)*:174-182, 1978.

Topol, Phyllis, and Reznikoff, Marvin: Perceived peer and family relationships, hopelessness and locus of control as factors in adolescent suicide attempts. *Suicide and Life-Threatening Behavior, 12(3)*:141-150, 1982.

Trautman, Edgar C.: Drug abuse and suicide attempt of an adolescent girl: A social and psychiatric evaluation. *Adolescence, 1(4)*:381-392, 1966.

Victoroff, Victor M.: A means of preventing teenage suicide. A psychiatrist discusses one solution. *Family Health, 9(4)*:22-24, 1977.

*Vital Statistics of the United States*. Washington, D.C., U.S. Department of Health and Human Services, Public Health Service, 1979.

Wenz, Friedrich V.: Economic status, family anomie, and adolescent suicide potential. *Journal of Psychology, 98(1)*:45-47, 1978.

What you can do. *Family Health/Today's Health*, April 1977, p. 24.

Zilboorg, Gregory: Considerations of suicide with particular reference to that of the young. *American Journal of Orthopsychiatry, 7*:15-31, 1937.

# GLOSSARY

*Adolescence*: the period from ages fifteen to twenty-four

*Attempted suicide*: an attempt to take one's own life voluntarily and intentionally without the attainment of death

*Caregivers*: physicians, psychiatrists, psychologists, nurses, social workers, therapists, educators, clergy, lawmakers, and counselors

*Committed suicide*: the act or instance of taking one's own life voluntarily and intentionally

*Intervention*: the treatment and care of suicidal crises or suicidal problems

*Lethality*: the probability of an individual committing suicide in the immediate future

*Postvention*: the process of helping survivors deal with the feelings associated with a suicidal death

*Prevention*: methods or ways of trying to keep suicidal behavior from occurring

*Prodromal clues*: warning signals of potential suicidal behavior

*Suicidal*: marked by an impulse to commit suicide

*Suicidal behavior*: threatened suicide, attempted suicide, or committed suicide

*Suicidology*: the scientific study of suicidal phenomena

*Taboo*: a prohibition imposed by social custom

# SUBJECT INDEX

# NAME INDEX